KEEPER OF SECRETS

PALMETTO
PUBLISHING
Charleston, SC
www.PalmettoPublishing.com

Copyright © 2024 by Wendy B. Mattell

All rights reserved

No portion of this book may be reproduced, stored in a retrieval system, or transmitted in any form by any means– electronic, mechanical, photocopy, recording, or other–except for brief quotations in printed reviews, without prior permission of the author.

Paperback ISBN: 979-8-8229-4774-0
eBook ISBN: 979-8-8229-4775-7

KEEPER OF SECRETS

WENDY B. MATTELL

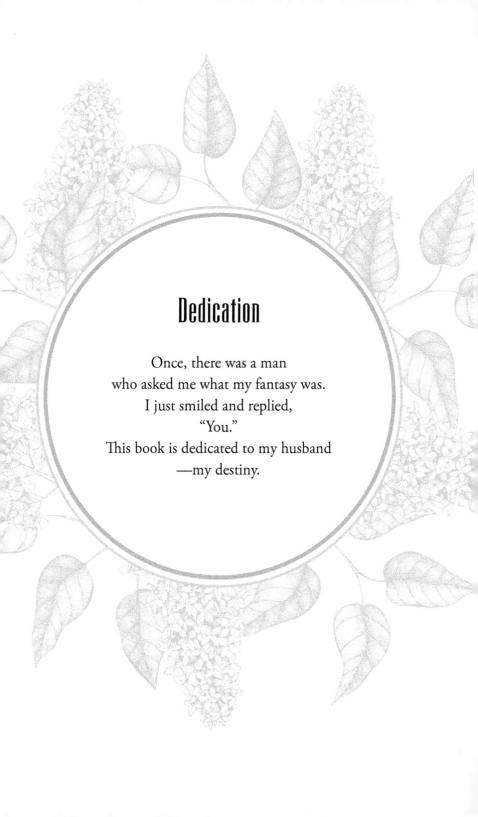

Dedication

Once, there was a man
who asked me what my fantasy was.
I just smiled and replied,
"You."
This book is dedicated to my husband
—my destiny.

Keeper of Secrets

The nightmares began coming more frequently. I was haunted by things I was convinced I had tucked deep down inside. Memories began escaping my subconscious as I slept. My thoughts began to resemble the broken pieces of glass inside a kaleidoscope. Memories began coming back to me like a jigsaw puzzle with pieces missing. Echoes of threats from long ago rang in my ears, and feelings of guilt and shame began creeping into my thoughts.

I woke suddenly; fear filled my mind, and my heart was pounding. It was dark, and I was out of breath. I was sweating as my heart raced with an overwhelming feeling of terror. It was irrational. I was home, safe in my bed. I reached over and felt the warmth of my husband's skin. The rhythmic sounds of his breath as he slept calmed me. I was safe.

It is time for me to tell my whole story in the hope that it will give others a space to feel safe talking about their stories. Ultimately, allowing myself and others to release the past and be able to move on and enjoy our lives.

The stories in this book are based on true events. Names have been omitted to protect the guilty and the innocent. These stories represent my journey from a loss of innocence far too young to finally and unexpectedly finding true love.

So, when I am an old lady sitting on my front porch with my friends, sipping a cocktail and sharing the stories of our lives, my stories will never begin with, I ordered a salad.

Christmas Spirit:
The Feeling of True Love

Excitement filled the air as the holiday season quickly approached. It was cold enough to see your breath, and snow was gently falling, causing a hush to fall over the yard. I watched as the trees began to look like they had sugar icing on their branches. Rays of sunlight sparkled like diamonds across the white blanket of snow on the lawn.

In the evenings, my family would ride around town, admiring the Christmas lights. People left their shades open so you could see the trees lit up and decorated with angels and stars at the top. The shopping plaza in town came alive, complete with a cage for Santa's live reindeer. There was a platoon of twenty-three toy soldiers strategically placed throughout the mall, standing ten feet tall. They had blue pants, a red jacket, and a tall blue hat with a feather. Positioned at their right hand was a shiny black rifle, ready to defend us. In the center of the courtyard stood the twenty-foot-tall general with the same uniform and a fancy feather on his hat, ready to command them. In the center of the courtyard were enormous wooden blocks that spelled out Joy to the World and a Christmas tree that stood over two stories high. Magic was in the air.

One of my favorite Christmas traditions was our family gift donation. My father's company sold gift sets to the major retailers this time of year. He always ordered extra sets so there would be enough to donate to the local churches.

Every year we set up a long table with brilliantly colored reams of wrapping paper and large rolls of scotch tape. Beside it, lay boxes upon boxes of gift sets. There were bath salts, sleeves of elegant soaps, and perfumed body powders with soft puffs and fragrances in fancy bottles nestled into gold foil packaging. There were also sets that had kid's bubble baths, character shampoo and conditioner, and bath toys. We spent a few hours every Saturday and Sunday wrapping until each gift was finished off with a beautiful bow and a tag. It read, From: Santa. I loved the idea of being one of Santa's helpers and imagined how happy the children or adults would be when they opened them to see the surprise waiting for them.

Two weeks before Christmas, we finished wrapping the last of the gifts and stacked them neatly in the living room when the doorbell rang. I stood behind my father as he opened the door. We were greeted by the chief of police. He was in full uniform and looked very stern yet friendly. Beside him there was a boy around my age. He introduced him as his nephew and the special helper to distribute the gifts. I smiled shyly at the tall, imposing man, shook his hand as I was taught to do when introduced to an adult, and said hello to the boy. He politely said hi and, as any ten-year-old boy would do, then proceeded to ignore me.

    I watched closely as they both made several trips in and out of the house, filling the back seat of the cruiser. When they came back in for the last boxes, they both thanked us for the gifts. This time the boy smiled at me as he said goodbye. I felt like we were connected, helping to bring Christmas cheer. The pure love and joy of the Christmas spirit filled every part of me. In my heart I felt that he had something to do with the spark of joy that touched me that day. I was convinced this was the feeling of true love, pure and unconditional.

    I often wondered what happened to that boy and his uncle, the chief of police. I don't remember ever seeing them stop by the house again. Every other year after that, we would wrap the gifts and deliver them to the local churches ourselves. He remained in my memory so clearly that I could recall his smile when I closed my eyes. I hoped that someday I would meet him again and perhaps find out why he had such an effect on me.

    I don't remember any gifts that were under the tree that year; only that feeling of pure, unconditional love and joy filled my heart. The fresh, crisp air allowing me to see my breath, the warm crackling fires, and the twinkling lights on the tree were my favorite gifts.

Loss of Innocence

The next year, my parents let my younger brother and I know that we would be having another person join our family. My mother explained that this boy was her half-brother and that his parents had passed away. She and my father planned on giving him a home and raising him. Although he was our uncle, we were to consider him to be like an older brother. My younger brother and I were very close before he arrived. After he came into our home, my younger brother preferred his company to mine. Our new uncle was sixteen, I was eleven, and my younger brother was eight. My younger brother was thrilled to have an older brother; they got along wonderfully, but there was something about him that made me feel uneasy.

My uncle had a bit of a mean nature toward me. Before bed he would tell me stories designed to frighten me. He seemed to take great pleasure in this and encouraged my younger brother to join in. As the boys began joining little league and football teams, I was feeling excluded. I was reminded by them as well as my parents that I was a girl and it was not appropriate for me to play these games. I began to feel quite invisible as I sat on the sidelines, expecting to cheer them on. I was offered ballet lessons in the fall and winter and swimming lessons in the summer.

I loved listening to the classical music played during dance class and my ballet teacher's instructions to feel the music and allow our bodies to move with it. I dreamed, as most little girls do, of becoming a ballerina, but in one of my lessons, I overextended one of my legs and pulled it so badly that I could not continue with classes. I was instructed to take warm baths with Epsom salts to help relax my muscles and heal my injury. My leg never healed completely, so once again, I became the audience for my uncle and brother.

I enjoyed the feeling of the warm, healing baths. Stepping out of a luxurious and relaxing bubble bath, feeling peaceful and full of joy, I wrapped myself in a warm, fluffy towel. One time, unknowingly, I opened the bathroom door to be greeted roughly by a pair of strong hands. It was my uncle. He grabbed me, dragged me across the hall, and threw me on the bed in the next room. At a time that should have been an age of innocence, it was suddenly and violently taken from me.

In seconds, my adolescent bliss leaped from joy to surprise and confusion, then quickly to fear. For a moment, I thought he was just teasing me to frighten me, but as he attempted to pull my towel from me, I realized he was not wearing any pants. My first thought was that he was angry with me for some reason, but he kept saying he wanted to show me how something worked. I was scared and began to cry for him to let me go. I called out for help, but we were alone in the house.

I tried to get away from him as I felt his powerful arms holding me down on the bed. I began kicking, and by chance, my knee caught him squarely and firmly in the groin. He doubled over in pain, releasing his grip enough so that I could escape. I hurried back into the bathroom and locked the door.

My heart was racing as tears stung my eyes and streamed down my cheeks. My ears filled with the sound of banging on the door and loud threats of payback that would come. I pulled the towel around my naked body and huddled as far away from the door as possible, waiting for the sound of the front door opening so that I would be rescued.

After what seemed like an eternity, I heard the sound of my mother's voice calling out hello as my parents came through the door. I flung the bathroom door open and ran down the stairs to my mother. With my heart racing and tears covering my face, I told her what had happened. She brought me to my room and stayed with me while I got dressed.

When we came down the stairs, my uncle and my father were seated at the kitchen table, chatting away, as if nothing had happened. I was, however, so hysterical that surely something had happened. My uncle remained calm and insisted that he had no idea what I was talking about. My parents were aware that he was having a difficult time processing his mother's death and decided it was time to seek professional help. They called a family therapist and made an appointment for the following week.

At the first appointment, the whole family was required to go. The therapist spoke with us individually. He had me go into his office first. I found myself sitting in a chair across a large, ornately carved wooden desk, with an intimidating, large, strange man sitting behind it. I felt small and frightened to be alone with this stranger. He spoke gently and encouraged me to tell him my side of the story.

As I recounted the events, the therapist listened and nodded occasionally with no expression. When I was done, he asked me what I thought had happened. I told him that my uncle was trying to force me to do things I didn't want to do. I was scared and uncomfortable talking to this strange man. He took a few notes and walked me out into the waiting room. I heard him tell my parents not to worry and that I was just fine. He recommended that my uncle have counseling to help him work through some issues. When we drove home, I sat quietly in the back seat next to my uncle, still scared and confused. I was far from feeling fine, but the conversation was over as far as everyone else was concerned.

After a short while, my uncle started to take revenge on me in small ways. He would sneak into my room before bedtime and lay in wait under my bed. Just as I was about to fall asleep, he would reach up and grab my face. During the day, when we were alone, he would brag about a new knife that he got and would menacingly show it to me. I became so frightened of him that I started sleeping on the floor at the foot of my parents' bed to feel safe.

My parents could not tolerate the upset in the house, and it was decided that my uncle would be sent to a private school. They felt it would be in everyone's best interest, and I felt relieved. I thought I would finally be safe.

The Boy Next Door

One day, soon after my uncle left for boarding school, there was a knock at the door. I went to open it, and there was his best friend. Assuming that he came to say goodbye, I told him that he had left already. He said he knew, and he knew why.

This friend stepped through the front door, put his hand over my mouth, pushed me into the hall closet, and told me to stay quiet. It was dark, and I felt his strong arms wrapped around my small body with his hand held tightly over my mouth.

I heard him whisper deeply and menacingly in my ear again, not to make a sound. He threatened that if I said anything to anyone about what he was going to do, people I loved would get hurt. I was terrified. I had no reason to doubt what he was saying, and I didn't know what he was planning on doing. I was too scared to move or make a sound.

He told me to tell my mom that we were going to the basement to listen to some music. As he led me down the basement stairs, she barely looked up from preparing dinner. Once downstairs, he informed me that we were going to play a game. He would tell me what to do, and I was to follow his directions.

He turned the music up so that nothing could be heard from the basement. He told me that I was to just lie down in front of him and not make a sound. I closed my eyes, trying not to cry, and did as I was told. I felt his hands touching my body in places I knew should not be touched. He left my clothes on, told me that he would be back the next day, and warned me again to keep quiet. He left me there on the cold basement floor. I listened as he went up the stairs, and I heard him say goodbye to my mom as he left the house.

The next time he came over, the reinforced threats that I was never to tell anyone or there would be consequences, were repeated. Truly frightened that I would be harmed or somehow hurt anyone else, I did as I was told and kept our encounters secret.

He began introducing me to various methods of foreplay, touching me in places that stirred feelings I truly did not understand. I was far too young to know what was happening. After the therapist and my parents' response to what happened with my uncle, talking about this subject was not an option, especially with the added threat of harm. Once again, I was left scared and confused, with nowhere to turn for answers.

His visits were almost on a daily basis, and he explored parts of my body I had not yet even discovered. He was beginning to awaken feelings and responses that I could not control or understand. I was frightened and confused. He did not remove my clothes, yet I felt naked before him.

After he was finished exploring me, he turned his attention to show me how to touch him. He guided my hands along the inseams of his jeans and then pressed my hand against the hard bulge in his pants. With a deeply lustful and husky voice, he told me to unbutton his jeans and unzip them. He was not wearing any underwear.

As he guided me to reach into his jeans, I felt his warm skin beneath my small hand. I noticed his breathing quicken as my fingers brushed against him. His erection was growing in response to my touch. He guided my hand carefully, slowly, and controlled up and down the shaft of his penis as it grew bigger and harder. I felt him start to speed up, holding my hand tighter and forcing my hand to follow his lead. Suddenly he came, hard. I had no idea what was happening. My young body was tingling in places I had never felt before. I felt confused, ashamed, and scared.

He told me I did well and that we would continue another time. He got up, put himself back in his jeans, and left me sitting once again on the cold basement floor alone. My mind was racing, and what should have been a time of innocence and discovery was taken from me in a matter of moments. I did not have a chance of discovery, but more of an education in the art of pleasuring his dominant male desires.

The next time he came over, instead of just running his hands over my clothes, he began to lift up my shirt and unzip my pants. He told me to stay quiet as his finger reached into me, exploring my untouched body. He started to touch me gently at first, then became more urgent and thrust his fingers deep inside me. It hurt and felt strange, and all the while, he was warning me to stay quiet. As my small body climaxed, he removed his fingers and left.

I had no idea what just happened. I felt so many emotions running through me: fear of people I loved getting hurt, excitement that I had never experienced, confusion, guilt, and shame. What had started with my uncle was happening again. I could not tell my parents; they had already told me that the doctor said I was fine. These were the adults and authority figures in my life. I was convinced that I was damaged—broken beyond repair. The only thing I could do to stay safe was to continue to keep the secrets no child should ever keep.

The clandestine meetings occurred nearly every day for five years. He would either come to my house or he would summon me to his. I became submissive and obedient. It was constantly reinforced that if I didn't do as I was told, people I loved would come to great harm. There was no way for me to know that his threats were empty.

Our interactions never went beyond touching him, practicing his techniques on my young body, and instructing me in ways to pleasure him. He never kissed me and never entered me. He technically left me a virgin, but not innocent. I felt used, broken, and confused. I was convinced no one would ever want or love me.

As the years passed, my body began to develop as well as my own desires. I had grown a strong libido and dreamed of the innocence of romance that I had been robbed of. My understanding of sexuality was tainted by my experiences as a child. I grew up in a family with all boys and in a neighborhood with only a few girls who were older than I was and had no interest in being my friends.

I listened to girls my age talking about boys they liked, the thrill of a first kiss, and the fantasy of having a boyfriend. I would sit quietly and wonder what it would have felt like to be simply and innocently kissed. I was unable to share my experiences for deep fear of harm coming to my loved ones and the true fear that I had developed of being judged.

I knew that what had happened and was happening to me was wrong, and I had been convinced that it was somehow my fault. My body was now responding to the lessons I was learning. I had no idea how to determine what was and was not appropriate behavior. The messages of my childhood experiences were mixed up, and there was simply no one to ask.

When I was thirteen, my parents told my brother and me that instead of celebrating Christmas at home, we were all going on a family vacation to Hawaii! I was so excited. My first thought was how exciting it would be to go to this magical place, and I would be out of the neighborhood and away from the boy next door for two glorious weeks, no one looking over my shoulder, feeling tense each time the doorbell rang. I would know what it would be like to be carefree.

Then, I heard my mother say, "And the best part is that our next-door neighbors would be coming also."

I could hardly believe my ears. My heart sank, and I fought the urge to burst into tears. Silently in my mind, I was screaming no, this cannot be happening. Everyone was so happy and excited that I knew the only thing I could do was lock my secret securely away, put on a smile, and join in the celebration.

When we arrived, my younger brother and I shared a room, I hoped it would offer me some form of protection. The neighbors had a boy his age, and they were friends. We were told to go ahead, explore the resort, and have fun; we were given a time to all meet back at the room, and everyone went their separate ways. I watched as the boy next door walked to the beach. I began to hope that he would be distracted by all the scantily clad girls his age at the beach and by the pool area. My brother and his friend went in the opposite direction, and my parents and their friends headed towards the pool bar. I was left on my own.

After a short time, I met a girl my age who was staying at the resort with her parents. We became fast friends as we explored areas of the resort together. It was so nice to have a girl my age to chat and giggle with.

One evening my new friend told me that there was going to be live music that night on the pavilion. Although we were not old enough to be in the seating area, we would be able to hear it from a spot she found tucked away on a path nearby. It sounded fun and exciting, so I agreed to meet her after dinner when my parents went out for the evening with their friends.

I was supposed to stay in my room after a certain time, but the thrill of sneaking out to listen to the music got the best of me. We met at the designated spot on the path and hid in the bushes so no one could see us. The music had just begun when suddenly I heard familiar voices. My parents and their friends were walking down the path directly towards us.

Before I had a chance to hide, my mom spotted me tucked away in the bushes and very sternly ordered me to come out. I knew from the tone of her voice that I was in a world of trouble. They silently escorted me back to my room and told me that I was grounded for the remainder of the trip. I could go to the beach or pool during the day, but after dinner each night, I had to stay in my room. I was strictly forbidden to have my new friend visit in the evening.

The next night, after dinner, my younger brother and his friend went out to explore, leaving me alone. There was a knock on the door just moments after he left, and I thought that he had forgotten his key. I opened the door, and there he was, the boy next door. He casually strolled into my room and told me to close the door and bolt it. Once again, I was under his control. He warned me that just because we were away from home, the rules had not changed. I was trapped.

Each night after dinner, my parents escorted me to my room, and my brother went out with his friend to explore. I sat on the bed, dreading that knock on the door. Some nights the knock did not come, but I was always on guard, my stomach in knots and my heart racing. For the next two weeks, I would sit by the open window, listening to people joyously chatting and enjoying their vacations.

I left my window open each night as I drifted off to sleep listening to the soft, lilting sounds of Hawaiian music in the not-too-far distance and the peaceful sound of ocean waves rhythmically rolling onto the shore. The air smelled clean and fresh as gentle breezes would caress my face. I closed my eyes and imagined that I was a part of this beautiful paradise, carefree and happy, but it was just a dream.

Deep down in my heart, there was one thing I knew was certain: I was an undying romantic. I loved the idea of love. I fantasized about one day being discovered, saved, and protected by the man who saw me, all of me, and loved me anyway. I believed the fairy tales young girls are told, that "someday my prince would come." Someone who would allow me to feel safe and secure instead of imprisoned and controlled.

I vowed at that young age, in my paradise prison, that although I had promised to keep the vow of silence to protect my loved ones, I would learn to control how my body responded to the "daily encounters." I began to observe the subtle and not-so-subtle reactions and responses to my touch as well as my responses to being touched. I developed the ability to restrain my own physical responses and vowed that I would always maintain that silent power over my own desire and ultimate release. This was the one secret that I kept, and that was mine and mine alone.

I discovered my own desires and ways to release my own sexual tension in the safety and solitude of my own room. I was determined to hold on to the one sacred act of love I hoped someday I would find. I decided that it would be my choice and decision when I would give that part of myself to another.

Over time, I became an astute student and, without realizing what was happening, became adept at the art of seduction and the ability to bring him to climax without him ever entering me. Our times together never went beyond touching. There was no tenderness or even kissing. I remained a "virgin" in the dictionary definition, yet I was not innocent. I was convinced that I was damaged, broken, and unlovable.

Searching for guidance, I attempted to bring up the subject of sex and relationships with my mother without telling the actual secret of my experiences. I remember being in the front seat of the car, sitting at a red light, and without taking her eyes off the road, she said to me, "You can't rely on your looks, so focus on your school work." My teenage ears heard that I was not very attractive, so I had better be sure that I had good grades. She promptly changed the subject to my schoolwork. This conversation left me feeling more hopeless than I had already felt. Once again, I tucked my secret deep down inside, where it would remain untold.

Innocence in Italy

When I was fourteen, my family took a "generations" trip to Italy. After a long flight from Boston, we finally arrived in Rome. I was so tired that I could barely keep my eyes open on the bus. I leaned my head against the cool glass of the window and listened to the repetitive sounds of the wheels rolling down the road as the bus gently rocked from side to side. Soon I fell into a gentle twilight sleep.

Suddenly I heard loud beeping and yells, coming from a car driving along the side of the bus. I looked down and saw a convertible filled with young men wanting to know if we were from America. I smiled and waved at one of the boys as the tour guide continued talking about the agenda for the rest of the day.

When we arrived at the hotel, we all checked in and decided to take a much-needed nap before meeting once again in the lobby for dinner. I went downstairs only to see the same young man who was in the car. He was chatting with the person behind the desk. He broke into a sweet, warm smile when he saw me and said hello in broken English. I smiled and then thought it best to walk away and find my family. He seemed very charming and attentive in a way that made me feel quite on guard.

He followed me, approached my family in the lobby, and introduced himself. He went to the eldest male, my grandfather; they said something to each other in Italian. After a short conversation with my grandfather, he had his permission to take me for a short walk to the square. He was to come back after the family had dinner, and then he gave the young man his room number and a time to return.

After dinner, the whole family was gathered in my grandfather's room when there was a knock on the door. The young man arrived on time with a bottle of wine and a beautiful bouquet of flowers. I invited him in, and once again he walked straight to my grandfather and handed him the wine, and then he found my mother and handed her the bouquet of flowers. My grandfather said something to him again in Italian, then in English, "You understand? She is back in her room by 8:00 p.m., not a moment later." The young man said he understood.

We had a quiet walk to the Trevi Fountain. He handed me a coin and turned me so my back was facing the fountain. He said, "Make a wish," and gestured for me to throw the coin over my head into the fountain. I made a heartfelt wish and tossed it in.

In the square there were a number of small restaurants and a gelato shop. It was my first taste of this amazing desert. As we continued walking and enjoying our gelato, it became clear we had some issues communicating , as I didn't speak Italian, and his English was limited to "Do you know Bob Dylan?" and something about owning a pizza parlor.

We were back at the hotel and outside my door a few minutes before 8:00 p.m. As we approached the door, he leaned in and kissed me on the lips. His kiss was sweet and gentle. It felt like a stolen kiss, as seconds later my grandfather opened the door to greet us. We said good night. That night as I lay down to sleep, I felt quite smitten with this handsome, charming, sweet Italian boy. This was my first experience with a boy who treated me with respect and kindness.

The next day we left for our next destination on the tour. As the bus was leaving, I looked out the window, and there he was, smiling and waving goodbye. Warm feelings toward this stranger rose in my heart. I smiled and waved goodbye as the bus pulled away.

Seven days later, we returned to the same hotel in Rome the day before our journey back to the United States. As the bus pulled in front of the hotel, I noticed him standing there, holding a beautiful bouquet of flowers. As I stepped off the bus, he came over, and this time he handed them to me.

He invited my family for lunch at his family's pizzeria before we left for the airport. The pizza was amazing. He asked for my address so he could write to me to practice his English. I handed him a piece of paper with my address written on it, and he gave me a warm, sweet hug, goodbye, and a kiss on the cheek. I thought it would be fun to have a pen pal.

We wrote for a few months, and one day I received a small package that contained a ring with a note that asked me to accept the ring as a promise to "marry him." The note read, "We can live in Rome and someday own the family pizzeria." I was stunned. Clearly things were done much differently in Italy than they were at home.

Although this was an incredibly romantic gesture, the reality was that, at the age of fourteen, that was not something I was interested in. I returned the ring with a letter saying that, though I was truly honored by his proposal, I would have to say no. I never heard from him again, and though I missed hearing from him, I understood.

This short and sweet romantic interlude was my first glimmer of hope that there was a future where I was more than a "practice thing" for the boy next door. I will forever hold the sweet romantic memory of this young boy in my heart.

My First Love

The boy next door finally left for university, and I had just entered high school. Finally, I thought, new beginnings. It was the first time in years that I could rest easy enough that the bell would not ring, and I could finally have some peace.

After a few months of adjusting to high school, it happened. I saw him across the room, and it was as if I were thunderstruck. There was an angelic look about him. Blond curls framed his face, and his eyes seemed to twinkle as his light and easy laughter called to me from across the room. Everything about his looks was opposite of the boy next door. He was just a few years older than me, and when he noticed me gazing at him from across the room, he flashed a sparkling smile at me that caused my young, hopeful heart to leap. He was so charming that it caught me off guard.

We met and sat together, chatting during lunches, and after a while, he asked me out on a date. I had actually never been on a date, except for my evening stroll in Italy. He picked me up, and we spent the evening driving around chatting and getting to know each other. When he dropped me off at my house, he walked me to my door and gave me a sweet good night kiss. My heart leaped with joy at the innocence of the evening. I was still dealing with the feelings of guilt and shame from the past five years of my secrets. Each time these thoughts came bubbling to the surface, I stuffed them back deep down into my soul, vowing not to let them spoil my chance of having a normal relationship.

After a few months of dating, he asked me if I would be his girlfriend. I was so thrilled to think that someone found me worthy of being with them. I thought for sure I was finally safe.

Our young relationship progressed, and we spent time getting to know each other and exploring sexual boundaries and desires. I did my best to keep the secret of my experiences and allow him to lead me and let me know what he liked. I had enough experience at this point to know how to be submissive without truly losing control.

There were times that it became obvious that he was not as experienced as the boy next door, and I unconsciously guided him in the directions I knew to be pleasurable. I did my best to allow him to feel that he was the one in control, as it seemed that he, like the boy next door, was most comfortable with that scenario. I assumed at this point that this was simply a male trait.

During the holiday break, my family was on vacation in Florida. One day the phone rang; it was the boy next door. He tried to pick up where he had left off with me, starting with the reinforcement of the threats of telling anyone about our "relationship." I informed him that I had a boyfriend now, and he could no longer see me. I threatened to tell my boyfriend what he did if he didn't leave me alone. For the first time, he did not threaten me or argue. I finally felt free of him.

Of course, I would never tell my boyfriend or anyone else what had happened. It was all too confusing and shameful. Although I was a virgin, I had more experience than girls my age should, and I was far more in touch with my own sensuality than would have been considered appropriate.

The following spring my boyfriend asked me to the senior prom and then invited me to spend the night and join the rest of his group of friends on a traditional trip to the cape the next day. I told my parents that I was staying at a friend's house after the prom and that a group of us would be going to the beach the next day.

We had been together for over a year. He convinced me of his love for me, and I was certain his love was true. I felt safe with him and decided he would be the one I offered myself to. I recall the sweet fantasies of romance that flooded my mind. I was certain that my first time making love would be as sweet, caring, and romantic as he had been during the long nights spent exploring each other with sweet innocence. He would take his time bringing me to the edge, caringly and lovingly. How could I have thought anything else?

After the prom he brought me home and unceremoniously unzipped my dress. He barely kissed me before he had me down on his bed. There was very little foreplay or care taken at all to be sure my body was ready to be entered. It was quick and painful raw sex; his lack of experience was somewhat shocking to me. He was rough and selfish, and he did not seem to care that this was my first time. There was no tenderness in his touch, just a young boy's desire to get laid.

As he started to enter me, I felt my delicate insides begin to tear. It hurt, and when I cried out in pain for him to stop, he just ignored me. He had no self-control or desire for anything except his own pleasure. He came fast and hard into me. Silently in the dark, tears streamed down my cheeks, and I became terrified, realizing that he had not stopped to use any protection. I was once again frightened and felt very alone. I lay awake as I listened to him fall into a deep, self-satisfied sleep.

The next day we were picked up by a carload of kids, and we all went off to the cape. I was sore, exhausted, and upset. This was his graduating class, and I really didn't know that many people. He was off most of the day, partying with his friends, and really not paying any attention to me. Hurt and scared, I just sat on the beach and waited for the day to end. When I finally got home, I took a long, hot bath, went to bed, and cried myself to sleep.

We had a long talk about how he treated me, and I told him that I was truly hurt. He apologized and held me the way he did before we had sex, with what my young and hopeful heart believed was love and care. I so wanted his words to be true that I pushed away any other thoughts.

I agreed to go on the pill, and he promised he would take things a little slower the next time. I chose to forgive the cruel way he had treated me on prom night, and again, I convinced myself he was just partying too much. I forgave him and, once again, opened my heart to him. Shortly after he graduated, he enlisted in the Air Force. He told me that he asked his friend to look out for me and kissed me goodbye.

A group of his friends used to gather at his best friend's apartment. I became friends with his sister, who was part of the group, and I was invited in. One night, I had done a little too much partying to drive home, so I asked if I could stay a little longer. His friend said it was no problem. I knew this to be my boyfriend's close friend, whom he had asked to look out for me, so I felt safe.

After everyone left, we were sitting on the couch, watching TV; I began to relax when suddenly he leaned over and began kissing me. I was taken by surprise, and before I could stop him, he pushed me down on the couch, pulled up my dress, and pulled down my underwear. Unceremoniously, he unzipped his pants and pushed himself inside me. I felt him slamming into me, and, within a few moments, he came deep and hard inside me. I was shocked. What the hell just happened? I tried to think of what it was that I did to make him think he could do that.

The words screaming in my mind—my boyfriend said to look out for me—came out.

He corrected me, saying, "No, he told me to watch out for you. He told me how hot you could be."

It felt like a lightning bolt had shot through my head. I felt betrayed and hurt. Once again, I was passed on to a best friend. I believed all the lies he told me, and I was truly devastated. This convinced me that I was surely unlovable. After years of conditioning, abuse, and my first encounter with sex,

I thought this must just be the way things were. I truly did not understand.

All I could think of was how horrible I must be to be treated that way. I felt dirty, ashamed, and afraid. Convinced I was to blame, I began to shut down. There was no one I could talk to, no one knew my story, and I was becoming a master at keeping secrets.

I could not let my pain show because if anyone had asked what was wrong, I couldn't tell them without breaking the rules that had been so masterfully ingrained deep into my very being. I continued to smile until it became my mask.

The Good One

The beginning of the new school year brought new classes and new faces. There was one boy who caught my eye. I noticed him watching me as I passed by his locker each day. There was a lighthearted energy about him that made me feel comfortable. He had beautiful, thick brown hair and chocolate brown eyes that were kind and gentle. I could not help but smile every time I saw him.

One day, as a joke, I walked over to him and said, "You know, there are rumors going around that we are dating."

He smiled, gave me a big bear hug, and said, "Let's give them something to really talk about." We dated for two years. He was sweet and caring, and he was truly one of the most amazing human beings I had ever met. His dad had passed away, and his mom was raising four kids on her own. We helped his mom care for his brothers and sisters after school and at night when she was attending night school. I enjoyed the closeness and love that were in this family.

I was falling madly in love with him, but the secrets and memories of my past kept me feeling utterly undeserving of this man. The betrayal of my first boyfriend as well as the shame and confusion of my experiences with my uncle and the boy next door, silently haunted me. I was convinced that there must be something wrong with me, or those things would never have happened.

He deserved a woman as wonderful and kind as he was. I was convinced it was not me. He didn't know that I was damaged by the secrets that started in the closet all those years ago. Secrets that made me question whether anyone would truly want or love me if they knew.

When it was time for him to graduate, he asked me out for a fancy dinner. After dinner, he presented me with a small diamond ring and asked me to marry him. He caught me totally off guard. All I could think of was that I had to protect this man from the mess that I was. He didn't know that I was not worthy of his pure, untainted love. I told him I loved him, but I would have to say no. He was looking to start his own family, and I had not even graduated from high school yet. I felt the weight of my secrets pressing down on me and heard the small voice in the darkness of my mind whispering that I was damaged and unworthy. I felt my heart ache, believing that I did not deserve to be with him.

He told me to keep the ring; he bought it for me and didn't want it back. To me, this small, perfect diamond represented hope that there were truly good people in the world, and I had been loved by one of them.

A few years later, I had the diamond reset as a stud earring. After drinking half a bottle of Southern Comfort, my roommate used an ice cube and a sewing needle to pierce a second hole in my left earlobe. The moment I heard the skin in my earlobe pop and felt the needle pass through, I handed the earring to my roommate, and it has stayed there ever since.

The Fantasy Man

When I turned eighteen, my father began taking me to business functions. He was grooming me to take over his company, and this was a sort of coming out and introduction to industry captains. One by one, I was introduced to powerful men from across the country. I felt intimidated in the company of these men, but I wore my well-practiced smile and politely listened to them. They were all very respectful and kind to me as we made light conversation.

One afternoon I was introduced to a man who created a storm inside of me just by looking in my direction and smiling. He was heartbreakingly handsome. His hair was black as coal, and his eyes were the color of the sky. When he smiled, it seemed as if the room had become a little brighter.

He was tall with strong looking shoulders and a perfect European physique, with his slender waist forming a perfect v-shape. His clothes looked as if they were tailored uniquely for him. He was quite a bit older, very distinguished, and what I thought to be the epitome of elegance. I was affected by his mere presence, and a simple smile from him caused me to blush.

The last night of the convention was reserved for the semi-formal cocktail party. It was a chance to dress up beautifully and listen to a live band. They played the kind of music that called for slow, romantic dancing. I sat alone at my table while my father was off talking with his peers, and I watched as men led their partners around the dance floor. The women's beautiful dresses swayed gracefully as they were guided across the dance floor. Mesmerized by the music and the beauty, I saw, out of the corner of my eye, my fantasy man walking my way. He asked if I would honor him with a dance.

He offered me his hand and led me onto the dance floor. When we reached the center of the floor, he skillfully turned me to face him. In a single move, he took me in his arms and held me close enough for my head to comfortably rest on his shoulder, with my nose nestled in the nape of his neck. I remembered my ballet teacher telling me to feel the music. I felt myself relax into his embrace as our bodies effortlessly and gracefully moved to the music.

I was entranced by the feeling of being held in his arms as I breathed in the woody, sensuous fragrance of his cologne. I felt my entire being melt into his as I leaned my forehead against his warm, closely shaven face. He whispered in my ear how beautiful I looked, and I felt my heart skip a beat.

The music ended; he walked me back to my table and thanked me for the dance. I watched as he moved on to speak to other people at the party, and I was content. The memory of this one dance will always be a perfect moment in time.

I began attending that convention every year with my father. Each year, I would wait for him to find me and offer his hand. He would respectfully guide me to the center of the floor. For just a few minutes each year, I would find myself in the arms of a man who made me feel special and safe. This would be forever engrained in my memory as a perfect moment in time.

Lessons Learned Not on the Curriculum

My first semester at university had started, and accounting was on my list of class requirements. I have never been great with numbers, and I was not looking forward to this class. I made sure that I got a seat in the front row so that I would have to pay attention.

While waiting for the professor, I could hear a distinctive sound of boots coming down the empty hallway just before he entered the room. He was six feet tall, with a slender build, dark wavy hair, and striking green eyes. He hung his brown leather jacket on the back of the chair, and lessons began. He had a strict and intimidating manner as he set before us the curriculum and requirements.

As I had feared, within weeks, I was falling behind. He offered time after class for questions, and I stayed with a number of other classmates. He worked with each of us individually and assured us that he was happy to work with anyone who needed it. I began staying regularly with a few others. He called on each student, answered their questions, and then dismissed them. I began to notice that, no matter who was there, I was always called last.

One afternoon, I took my seat after class and began waiting for my turn. He walked over to me, and asked me to hold his jacket. I noticed how soft and buttery the jacket felt, combined with the warm, earthy aroma of the leather, it was intoxicating. I sat, patiently holding his soft, well-worn jacket in my hands. The other students finished their questions and left before he called me up to his desk.

After he answered my questions, he invited me to the school pub for a beer. He said he was meeting a friend, and if I was interested, he would like me to join them. I thought, *well, I have no more classes; it's Friday, why not?*

As we entered the pub, he was greeted by a man, a tiny bit taller than him, with a booming, "Hi, over here!" We joined him at his table and ordered a round of beers. We played a few games on the pinball machine and drank another round. It turned out that this man was his best friend. Everything about him seemed in direct contrast to my professor; his dirty blond hair was wild, and his eyes were the color of the ocean. Although they were nearly the same height, he was more muscular yet still slender. We all enjoyed our beer and talked, and it became very clear that it was not only their looks that were contrasting; their personalities were also quite different.

My professor was very measured and controlled in his speech and actions. He had a cool kind of mystery about him. The way he presented himself projected a confidence that was very attractive and strangely exciting. He sat beside me in the booth, and I could feel the warmth of his body close to mine.

His friend appeared to be more free-spirited, warm, and affectionate. He had a quick smile and a booming laugh that was contagious. The two of them bantered easily, the way friends who have known each other for years do. They made me feel welcomed and comfortable.

I was invited again to have beers at the pub with them after class the next week. I had so much fun the week before that I didn't even hesitate. As we were sitting at the table, my teacher's friend went to buy us our first round of beer, and my teacher asked me if I had a pack of cigarettes with me. I did, and he asked me to pull it out.

He told me that he had an assignment for me. He took a pen and inscribed his initials in a specific monogram style on the upper right corner of the logo of the pack. He then instructed me to take the pen and trace it until I felt that I could reproduce it on a napkin.

I thought this was a bit odd, but strangely interesting. I sat and traced that monogram until I felt it was perfect. I reached over and took a new napkin, traced it, and then handed it to him. I had no idea where he was going with this.

He looked at my replication of the initials and seemed pleased. We all enjoyed our beer, and I sat quietly, listening to their playful banter. I found myself feeling quite comfortable in the company of these two men.

His friend went up to get another round, and my professor turned to me, put his hand on my cheek, and kissed me on the other cheek gently and sweetly. I felt a catch in my breath as he leaned towards me, those gorgeous green eyes looking into mine. I felt as if he could see into my soul.

His friend came back, and the professor leaned back in the booth as if nothing had just happened. My head was spinning. Just before we left the pub, the professor told me that each time I bought a new pack of cigarettes, he wanted me to put his monogram in the corner, just as he had done with my pack, and that he would check each week to see if I had done it. He made it sound like a homework assignment, then leaned forward and kissed me gently on the cheek again.

His tender playfulness made me feel very special. I agreed that I would place his monogram on every pack of cigarettes I purchased. It appeared to me at the time to be a wildly romantic request. The next week when we met, he asked to see my cigarette box and seemed pleased to find his monogram flawlessly inscribed exactly the way he had requested.

The next week after class, he told me that he was interested in seeing me outside of the class without his friend. If I agreed, however, there would be rules:

No one was to ever know about us. (I was well versed in keeping secrets, so this was not a problem.)

He would be harder on me than my classmates.

He expected all assignments for his class and every class to be completed before I could see him.

He would call me to arrange times for us to meet.

After I agreed to all of the conditions listed above, he walked me to my car and assured me that he would call soon. I spent every moment doing my homework and preparing for our first date while I waited for his call.

When he finally called, his first questions were about my homework assignments. After I assured him that my work was complete, he gave me the day and time that he would pick me up. My heart was racing, and I was feeling anxious and excited. It was our first time alone. He was intensely curious and asked me a lot of questions about my plans for the future and the things I was interested in. He never talked about himself.

At the end of the night, he opened the car door for me, offered me his hand, and as I stood up, he pulled me into his arms. He closed the door and pressed me up against the car. His body was fully pressed against mine as he leaned down and gave me a deep, warm, passionate kiss. I felt as if the pressure of his body against mine was holding me up. My legs were weak, and if he had backed up, they may have betrayed me.

He slipped his arm around my waist and walked me to my apartment. I felt as if time had slowed down. I opened the door, and he silently followed me in. The apartment was dark, and my roommates were not home. He took my hand, led me to my room, and closed the door.

He pressed his mouth against mine as he started to take off my clothes. Slowly he unbuttoned my shirt, and then he reached around my waist and released my skirt. My clothes dropped to the floor. I was left standing in front of him, nearly naked. He undid my bra and slipped it off. He sat me down on the bed as he slid his hands into my underpants, slipping them over my hips, down my thighs, off one foot, and then the other.

He laid me down on the bed and began to unbutton his shirt. Holding my gaze with his piercing green eyes, he took off his clothes in the same slow, seductive way that he had disrobed me. I admired his smooth, well-toned chest and his strong arms. He was very tall and lean. His stomach was tight and flat. He was perfectly toned and truly gorgeous.

As he took off his pants, he laid his body against mine, pressing me into the bed. I could feel how hard and warm he was. I reached out to touch him, but he stopped me. He ran his fingers slowly over every curve on my body. He began kissing the nape of my neck, and I felt my heart pounding as I became breathless and wild with desire.

He then made his way down my body, first with his hands, then his mouth, circling my breasts with his hands, but he did not touch my nipples. He gently kissed my breasts, and he kept moving his hands down my body. He caressed my stomach, kissing me as he ran his hands once more down my hips, then up my thighs.

He was driving me crazy with desire. I wanted more of him. Then he reached around and took my ass in his hands. He lifted me up and sat me in his lap with my legs wrapped around his waist. It was the first glimpse I had of him, fully naked. He was hard and hot. He positioned himself so that, as he lifted me onto his lap, he brushed himself across me and felt just how hot and wet I was. He was just teasing me. He kept me in a position where I was in his complete control. My body was responding wildly with the desire to feel him inside me.

He smiled at this, leaned his head down, and slowly and mindfully took each nipple in his mouth. He took his time as he focused his attention on how I reacted to a little more pressure. I began wriggling around, my breath began to quicken, and I became frenzied with desire. He reached down and slid his fingers into me. First one, then two; he moved slowly at first to see how I would respond. My body locked onto his fingers, begging for him to go deeper and move faster. Once again, he smiled that seductive, confident smile I had begun to recognize. He was pleased. He was in control.

He gave me a small lift in the air and placed me on top of him. He was so hard, and I was so wet that he slid inside of me, filling me up just to the point of pain. One smooth glide, and he was deep inside me. My legs still wrapped around him, and he began lifting my body up and down in a slow rhythm that made my insides begin to quiver with excitement, and I was very near orgasm.

He began to thrust himself inside me; at first, slowly, I met the rhythm he set, and he began to speed up. As he thrust deep inside me, I felt him release, and at the same time, my body reached a wild orgasm. We stayed like that for a few minutes. After we caught our breath, he gently laid me down on the bed, got dressed, and kissed me softly on my forehead. He told me he would call soon. After he left, I fell into a deep, satisfied sleep.

Each week, he would call, and the first question would be, is all your work done? I always answered honestly, and if the answer was no, he would cancel our time together until I was done. I did the best I could to keep up with my assignments, as I was becoming quite fond of spending time with him.

It was made clear that it was in my control how often I saw him as long as I followed his rules. When I did, he would show up at my door and take me for lovely dinners, followed by amazing sex. He continued to check my cigarette packs, telling me that it showed him that he was in my thoughts. I began automatically inscribing his monogram on each pack of cigarettes as a kind of ritual. Perfectly placed and carefully repeated each and every time.

    Sometimes the sex was seductive, almost romantic; other times it was a little rougher. The one thing that never changed was that he was in control. It seemed normal to me for him to be in control. After all, this was how I was trained to please someone from a very young age. I learned not to question but to drop my eyes and listen to instructions. Depending on what he was in the mood for, he would set the tone. I became adept at being a good girl and doing as I was told. I knew that when he was pleased, everything would be fun and exciting. I began to have deep feelings for this man and believed he cared for me also. He was an authority figure to me, and I trusted him.

    He introduced me to his friends outside of the one I knew from the pub. I was invited to dinner parties and events. His friend from the pub and I grew closer as he was always there, and he was really the only one I was comfortable with besides the professor. Although everyone was kind, they were all much older than me, and I felt intimidated and insecure.

    As we sat in the corner together, his friend and I talked about books and life. He shared with me his interests and more esoteric topics than I ever discussed with the professor. This man was fascinating in his own right. He was truly a free spirit, and I was very comfortable in our friendship and began confiding in him. We chatted on the phone together, and he recommended books for me to read. Then, he would take the time to discuss them with me. I found his choice of books very interesting. Shogun and The Art of War by Sun Tzu were two that he was very keen on me reading.

The semester was coming to an end, and I was studying day and night to be sure that all my assignments were complete and I was ready for all my exams. I wanted to keep my GPA high, and I knew the rules of seeing my professor. We had not seen each other in a few weeks as I was preparing for exams, and he said he would not distract me and that he expected me to ace his final exam.

I was well conditioned after so many months to do as he said without question. I did not really give it a second thought; it had become somewhat second nature. When I felt that I was sufficiently ready for all my finals and all my assignments were complete, I let him know at class that week that I was ready.

He asked me to stay after class; he had something he needed to talk to me about. When everyone had left, he sat me down and told me that his ex-girlfriend was coming back to town and that they were getting back together. He was sorry, but he could not see me anymore. I was devastated, ex-girlfriend? I never heard a word about her. I was stunned and speechless.

I walked away; my heart was pounding and my vision blurred. What just happened? I had built my world around pleasing this man, and he was discarding me at a moment's notice. I was so furious, all I could think was that this did not end like this. He had put himself in total control, and I agreed to it because I trusted him. Well, I wasn't feeling very agreeable to anything that would please him at the moment. In fact, just the opposite, I wanted him to feel the same betrayal that I was feeling.

When I got home, I called his friend and told him what he had done and that I was hurt and angry. He told me he knew about the ex and thought what he did was really wrong. I asked him if he would be open to helping me give his friend a taste of his own medicine. He laughed that booming laugh that always made me feel comfortable, and he said, "Absolutely!"

I decided that the best way to repay this man's cruelty was to behave in the exact opposite manner in which he had trained me over the past few months. I made a hotel reservation, went to the nearest lingerie store, and bought myself a slinky, sexy outfit—one that made me feel powerful and in control. I called his friend and told him that I was going to pick him up and that we were going on an overnight together. I had made all the plans. His response—opposite of what the professor's would have been—was to be completely open to whatever I had in mind.

As we drove to the hotel, he asked what I had in mind. I told him that I wanted to have sex with him. I didn't want him to worry about strings or emotional attachments. I was honest with him and told him that, in my heart, this would be an act of pure revenge. I explained to him that it was important for me to be in control. He laughed and told me that he was fine with it all. When we got to the hotel, we both had a drink and relaxed together for a while.

I instructed him to take off his clothes, and he willingly obliged, giving me the opportunity to see him for the first time, not as a friend but as a lover. God, he was beautiful. His dirty blond hair was mussed and wild as he took off his shirt. He slid his pants down until they hit the floor. He kept those beautiful sea blue eyes fixed on me, waiting for instructions.

We took a long, hot shower. I soaped and caressed every inch of his strong back and perfectly rounded ass. I turned his body toward me, and he leaned in to kiss me. I told him, no. I wasn't ready; I would let him know. He simply smiled, closed his eyes, and completely surrendered to my touch as I continued to explore his body under the warm running water.

His excitement grew as I slid my fingers around him. I felt his body quiver a little, then I backed off. The night was young, and I was not done yet. We rinsed off, and I told him to grab a drink, and I would be right out.

I put on my new outfit. It was a red, low-cut lacey cat suit. The legs were French cut and rode high on my thighs. It made my legs appear longer than they are and hugged every curve of my body. My intention was to take back my personal power. I was not feeling romantic. I had hot, raw sex on my mind; I was feeling very sensuous, sexy, and vengeful. When I came out of the bathroom, I watched his eyes light up. He started to say something, and I put my hand up and shook my head no, letting him know I did not want him to speak. I needed to keep a tight grip on my goal and could not let my emotions get the better of me.

I kissed him for the first time, and his kiss set me on fire. He was warm, passionate, and gentle, yet urgent. I was immediately ready for him. I felt myself surrendering to his touch. This was happening too fast. I pushed his body gently away from mine and asked him to lay back and let me take control.

As he lay back on the pillow, I began kissing his neck and running my fingers over his shoulders. He was cut and strong, toned, and muscular. I ran my tongue down his stomach as my hands gently brushed over his thighs. I raised my hand up to cup his balls, leaned down, and slid him into my mouth. Just a little bit, enough to make him want more. He tried to push himself into my mouth, and I pulled away, giving him a warning look that told him no. This was all going to be at the pace I set. He was to control himself until I said it was time.

As he was lying back on the bed against the pillows, I climbed on top of him and pulled the bottom of the suit to one side. I began moving slowly along his hard pulsing cock, letting him feel how he was affecting my body. I reached down and put him inside of me. Slowly and carefully, I pressed my body down on him until he filled me up. I felt him grow a little more as he slid into me. My body began to shift and move in response to him inside me, tilting my pelvis back and forth in a slow rhythm that was pleasing to me. As my excitement grew, I shifted up on my knees and began to ride him. I was just about to reach a hard, strong orgasm, and I told him to cum with me. In a burst of passion, we both came long and hard. I collapsed into his arms, my heart pounding, and I was breathless.

Afterward, my emotions took over, and, as tears burned my eyes, I began to cry softly. He wrapped me tenderly in his arms and told me he thought what his friend did to me was wrong. He assured me that I did not deserve to be treated that way as we both fell into a light sleep, snuggled in each other's arms.

A short time went by, and I felt his hands tracing my body. He began to remove the lingerie that I still had on. I did not resist. As I lay naked before him, he leaned over me and kissed me sweetly. I felt him getting hard again and wondered if I would be able to take him into me again. He was larger than I was used to, and I was sore, but he took his time and waited for me to be ready. I realized that his intention was focused entirely on how I responded, not on what he wanted. He was in control; the difference was that he wanted to please me. He slid into me gently and slowly, just a little, and then withdrew; he brought me to the point of intense desire as he entered me, slowly, just a little more each time until he was deep inside me. Our bodies met fully in an intense climax. We fell asleep once again in each other's arms.

The next morning we showered separately and packed up, and I drove him home in silence. He asked if I was ok, and I told him yes. I warned him that it was my intention to tell the professor what we had done, and he understood. He asked what day and time my exam was and wished me luck.

I spent the next few days reviewing every lesson and studying for my accounting exam. I planned on getting an A not for the professor, but for myself. I walked into the classroom picked up my exam and barely looked him in the eye. Quietly, I sat in my seat and proceeded to answer every question with ease.

I was sure to take the entire hour and double check my work. I lingered as everyone slowly turned in their exams. I could feel his eyes on me. I smiled inside because I knew that I was about to say and do something so out of character for me and how he knew me. God, I was so damn angry. I needed to finish this on my terms.

I turned in my paper, and he asked me to wait for him. I still had not said anything, and, as we were walking towards the stairwell, I saw his friend slowly coming up the stairs. The professor started to say something about our relationship, and I stopped him. I said with coolness in my voice, "There is nothing left to say; we are done." Then I said, "There is one more thing: I spent the weekend in a hotel room, having hot, hard sex with your friend, and he was amazing."

His friend had reached the top of the stairs just in time to hear me and locked eyes with the professor. I watched as the professor processed what I had just said. His face turned bright red with rage, and I said, "By the way, I am sure I got an A on that exam, and it best be reflected on my report card." I turned my gaze to his friend and smiled as I started to walk down the staircase, leaving him and the professor at the top of the stairs.

The professor was speechless. I heard his friend call him out, then and there, on the stairwell, saying that this was entirely his own fault. His friend then told the professor that he had better grade me according to my work and not what happened between us. I felt vindicated, and a final rush of anger swept through my mind and my body. I walked down the stairs alone and out the door. I got an A on the final and an A for the class. I never spoke to either one of them again.

The Summer I Was a Fuller Brush Man

Just before summer break, my father informed me that it was time to think about beginning classes that would help me run the family business. Although I had attended a number of sales conventions with my father, I had not thought much about having a career in sales. So I decided to try my hand at selling Fuller Brush products.

For those who don't remember, the Fuller Brush Man (typically men, hence the term) would go door to door with a catalog and a sample bag filled with products from top-of-the-line hair brushes to various cleaning solutions and gadgets for the house to demonstrate and hopefully sell. I thought this would be a perfect summer job to introduce me to the world of sales since it was a full-service experience from demonstrations to delivery.

One of the hottest products I had was a hand held carpet sweeper. This wonderful product was new to the market, and I had nearly a 100 percent rate of sale each time I demonstrated it. I was canvassing neighborhoods near where I lived. As I walked from door to door, street by street, with the sample bag and the carpet sweeper in hand, I wondered if I would have any luck presenting my wonderful new product to a more professional market.

I walked into a car dealership down the street, thinking this would be perfect for their showroom. It was quiet that day, and I was lucky to have a few people willing to listen to my presentation. Not only was the owner of the dealership interested in purchasing a carpet sweeper for the showroom, but a few of the salespeople wanted to buy one for their own personal use as well. I happily took their orders and let them know that I would deliver them as soon as they came in.

As I was packing up my materials, one of the salesmen offered to carry my bags to my car. He was tall with dirty blond hair that framed his face. His stormy blue eyes, highlighted by a golden summer tan, were captivating. At first glance his suit and tie gave him an air of professionalism and were well-tailored, yet they seemed to strain slightly against his muscular build. He was tall and ruggedly handsome, with an alluring smile.

He opened my door for me and charmingly asked if he could take me to lunch sometime. I was absolutely taken back; this man was gorgeous. I could not fathom why he would be interested in me. Feeling a bit on the defensive from my last relationship, without thinking, I blurted out, with all seriousness in my voice, "I'm sorry, but I don't date ugly men."

The look of surprise on his face at my response was a little amusing. He shook his head slightly in what seemed like disbelief. I got into my car, closed the door, and rolled down the window.

I smiled sweetly at him and said, "I will contact you when your carpet sweeper comes in." He started to say something, but I just smiled again and shook my head a little as I drove away.

A week later, the orders came in. I had all the products customers had ordered during the week laid out on the floor and was filling them one by one according to my invoices. As I picked up the order form from the car salesman, I noticed that he had written his home phone number across the top. I called the number to let him know that his order was in and I would be delivering his carpet sweeper to the dealership that week. Once again, he asked me to lunch.

I laughed a little and playfully asked him, "Are you just not used to hearing no?"

He answered, "No, I am not."

His honest response made me laugh. I repeated that I would deliver his order and said goodbye.

When I delivered the orders to the dealership, he once again asked me to lunch. I had to give it to him; he was persistent, and so I agreed to have lunch with him.

He walked me to my car, and as he was about to close the door, he said, "There is just one thing that I need to tell you before our date." He hesitated for just a moment, then said, "This is not my only job; I am also an erotic dancer."

I wasn't sure I understood what he meant, so to clarify what I thought I heard, I said, "An exotic dancer?"

He corrected me, "No, erotic."

I honestly had no idea what he was talking about. He saw the confusion in my eyes, smiled mischievously, and said there was a difference, but did not elaborate. *Well, okay, then,* I thought, *one lunch.* I agreed to have him pick me up the next day at the office I was working from.

When he arrived I introduced him to some of the ladies in the office (I had not told anyone anything except that he bought a carpet sweeper from me) and was surprised by their reactions to him. In his very charming manner, he flashed a seductive smile, and as he shook each one of their hands, he looked deeply into their eyes, making them feel, one by one, as if they were the only women in the room for a moment in time. I watched as five middle-aged women melted and began giggling like school girls.

A moment later another one of the ladies, who was in the back, hearing the commotion, came to investigate. As she turned the corner, he looked up and smiled at her.

She blurted out, "Hey, I know you. Didn't I see you on TV? You were being interviewed about what it is like to be a male stripper for Play Girl Magazine."

He answered, "Yes, that was me," and he beamed with delight, like a celebrity being recognized by a stranger.

My mind was racing as I listened to them chat for a moment about the interview. I was still processing what it meant to be an erotic dancer, but now I found out he was in Play Girl Magazine. What was I getting myself into? We left shortly after with a chorus of ladies singing their farewell's, with a mist of fantasy in their eyes.

When we arrived at the restaurant, we were promptly seated in a cozy booth. The server came over to introduce herself and take our order. She took one look at him and immediately focused all of her attention on him. I felt as if I had suddenly disappeared. He gracefully shifted her attention towards me and my order first, placed his order, and off she went. I was beginning to understand his confusion at my initial refusal of his luncheon invitation. He really was not used to that kind of rejection, or perhaps any at all. Women were all but throwing themselves at him.

I asked him why he decided to become an erotic dancer. He told me that he was working to put himself through college; he was making good money and having fun. Weekends and weekdays at the car dealership and one or two evenings at the club covered the costs of school and living expenses. He told me he was a biology major and hoped someday to go to medical school. We sat for quite some time, enjoying our lunch and conversation.

When he dropped me off at the office once again, he invited me to come and see his show. He informed me that he was the center stage spotlight dancer. All I could envision was a bunch of drunk, horny women clamoring for the chance to stuff dollar bills into this man's G-string. I laughed a little and told him I was not interested in seeing that, and, in a playful way, I said that I would prefer a private viewing. If he wanted me to watch him dance, he would have to dance just for me. Never in a million years did I expect that his response would be that he would love to do that for me.

He offered to cook me dinner and give me a private show with a confident smile. What girl would refuse that offer? This whole thing seemed surreal. He wrote his address on a piece of paper and the time for me to arrive, and I agreed. He thanked me for a lovely lunch, told me he was looking forward to our dinner, and kissed me sweetly on the cheek.

He lived in an upscale apartment complex with a private pool and beautiful grounds. I knocked on his door, and he greeted me with a warm smile and a hug. The apartment was filled with wonderful aromas, and he had set a lovely table with candles lit and a bottle of wine. After we enjoyed a delicious meal, he poured me another glass of wine and invited me to sit with him on the couch. We sipped our wine and chatted easily with each other, with soft music playing in the background.

I began feeling relaxed from the wine and conversation. He stood up and took hold of my hand gently to bring me off the couch. He swept me into his arms, held me close and firmly to his body, and began to dance with me. As he began to guide me around the room with ease, I laughed lightly and playfully reminded him that he had invited me to see him dance.

He flashed that charming smile and, without a moment of hesitation, positioned me back on the couch for a perfect viewing and changed the music to a more sensual tune. As I watched him move to the music, his breathing and movements shifted into a powerful stance. I was witnessing him becoming the center stage attraction that earned him an interview and spotlight in Playgirl Magazine.

He slowly and seductively began moving his body to the music in perfect rhythm. He began unbuttoning his shirt slowly and deliberately, never taking his eyes off of me and watching my response. As each button was slowly released, I had my first glance at his well-defined muscles, smooth skin, and even golden tan.

Continuing to move tantalizingly to the music, he took his time, allowing me to fully admire his strong, muscular chest and arms. He slipped off his shoes and let his hands rest playfully on the top of his perfectly fitting jeans before unbuttoning them. I admired how seductively he moved, becoming one with the music. He slowly slid the zipper down, and I had a glimpse of his strong, tight stomach. He watched me closely, with a twinkle in his eyes, responding to my apparent enjoyment of his performance. He continued to slide his jeans easily and effortlessly over his hips, revealing his magnificently cut lower abdomen. I could not help but smile with delight as he removed his pants to reveal his perfectly sculpted body. It reminded me of a Renaissance painting, muscular and flawless. He was in that moment vulnerable as he stood naked before me, and I was captivated.

In a single movement, he swept me off the couch, cradling me in his arms; he carried me into the bedroom. He kissed me lustily, then laid me down on the bed, and began undressing me. He took the same care in undressing me as he did himself. I felt the cool air conditioning brush across my nipples when he removed my bra, and they became hard with excitement. He kissed me as he gently ran his fingers, then his hands over my breasts, sliding down my torso, as he unbuttoned my jeans.

In one sweeping and flawless motion he removed my pants, then my underwear, sat back, and smiled at me lying naked on his bed. He admired my curves and made me feel appreciated and beautiful as he pulled me closer to him.

I felt his body moving to the sounds of the music playing in the other room, and my body began to follow his lead. He was passionate and patient. He took his time with a slow hand and steady gaze, watching my every response. Masterfully he waited until just the right moment when I was nearly begging for him to be inside me. His movements were controlled and deliberate as he slid his fingers inside me, deeper each time, teasing me and nearly bringing me over the edge.

He skillfully and effortlessly flipped me off my back and sat me on top of him. I was straddled across his hips, and I suddenly felt the heat and hardness of him entering me. He slid himself fully inside of me and held me by my hips as he began moving faster, bringing us both to an explosive orgasm.

His strong hands held me in the position on top of him for a minute, and then he guided me down to the bed beside him as he once again cradled me in his arms. I felt his body relax, and his breathing became shallow as he drifted into a light sleep. I lay there, listening to his heart beat and feeling the gentle rise and fall of his chest. I was deliciously sore and satisfied.

We started spending time together during the day on his days off. He was on stage most nights, and I refused to go to his shows. I felt the same way as I did from the beginning; I didn't want to see drunken women climbing over themselves to get his attention. I saw that every day as it was and could only imagine what it would be like at the club.

As the weeks followed, we spent more and more time together. On sunny days, he insisted that we lay by the pool so that he could work on his tan. He wore bathing suits that barely covered his body to avoid tan lines. One day when I came over, he had a bathing suit for me. It was much more revealing than I would have bought for myself, and it was the same color as his.

He began making comments about my food choices and my wardrobe. He would choose outfits for me that he said flattered my figure. At first I thought it was sweet that he was paying such close attention to me. The only issue I had was his choice of clothing for me. They were styles that he enjoyed viewing more than ones that I was comfortable wearing. I went from feeling flattered to feeling like an accessory.

One day as I was heading to the gym, an activity that I truly enjoyed doing by myself, he asked if he could join me. He said he thought it would be fun to work out together. When we arrived, I told him that I had a routine that I was comfortable with and that he should feel free to do whatever workout he did. To my annoyance, he began following me around the circuit, criticizing my routine and wanting to create a new one for me. I asked him to please stop a number of times. He was relentless once again, showing me that he was in fact not accustomed to being told no. By the time we left the gym, I had come to the realization that our relationship, as it was, revolved solely around his pleasure.

Although he was a master of flattery and seduction, his true hedonistic and self-centered nature shone through. He had no interest in what I wanted, and I was not interested in seeing him any longer. I ended the relationship that afternoon.

At Duck Pond

At the end of the summer, a group of us gathered on the Cape, and we all headed out to a secluded spot called Duck Pond. It was located a short ride from the main road, down a small dirt road to a clearing. This clearing was where we would park our cars. From there we would walk down a winding path and through the woods, carefully stepping over roots. You could hear the calming sounds of birds singing as the smell of the trees and the earth filled your senses. The leaves offered shade and relief from hot summer days.

At the end of the path, there was a beautiful glacial lake sparkling in the sunlight with a small sandy area at the edge. The water was always clear and cool, and there were never very many people there. Any tension or stress you may have felt was always replaced with a sense of calm reassurance that all was right and beautiful in the world. It was a lovely sanctuary.

One day there was a larger group of people than usual, and we were all partying pretty hard. Day turned into evening, and it seemed as if the group was growing. The star studded sky was clear, but it was a new moon, so it was very dark closer to the trees. We were all relaxed and having a wonderful time.

    Suddenly a tall man emerged from the darkness behind me. No one could really tell who it was, but we were all friends, and he was greeted as such. Without warning he scooped me up in his arms and began carrying me down the path toward the parked cars. No one seemed to notice what was happening, and I started to object, then I yelled for him to put me down. Quickly he covered my mouth with his hand. He was very strong, and I was really scared. I tried to wriggle out of his grasp, but he held me tighter to his body until I could not move at all.

    He carried me past the area where we had all parked our cars farther down the path to his car, opened the door, and shoved me in the back seat. I tried to move to the other side to get out, and he caught me by the legs, pulled me back towards him, and turned me on my back. He told me to stop fighting him and to shut up, and I would not get hurt.

    He yanked my skirt up and ripped off my underpants. In a flash of searing pain, I felt myself tear as he slammed himself into me over and over again. When I tried to scream, he covered my mouth again and told me to shut up or it would get worse. I felt as if I were leaving my body as memories of being tossed in a closet flooded my mind. I could hear the words as clearly as if it were happening in the moment: keep quiet, and no one will be hurt. I went limp, hoping it would not hurt as much if I didn't fight and praying it would be over soon. I blacked out.

When I came back to my senses, I was sitting on the ground in a parking lot. I truly don't know how I got there, nor did I know where I was. The sun was just beginning to rise. I got up, straightened my skirt, and began walking. There was really only one main road; I would be able to find my way back to the house where I was staying. I kept walking in a daze until I found my way back to the house. No one was awake yet, so I just went into my room, laid on my bed, and fell into a fitful sleep.

My housemates began to wake up; I heard the familiar shuffling and hushed tones of people nursing their hangovers, discussing breakfast and the plans for the day. I was still numb from the night before; no one questioned that I had left before them. Still in shock I didn't say anything. After all, what would I say? I had no idea who the man was. He did not leave any visible marks on my body. I could hear the boy next door's voice from childhood ringing in my ears: Don't say anything to anyone, and no one will be hurt. My mind was swirling, trying to make sense of what happened. Everyone just assumed that I was hung over and had a late night, and I simply kept quiet.

After that night, anytime anyone wanted to go to Duck Pond I came up with a reason why I could not make it. I simply could not bring myself to drive down the small dirt road that would take me to the once magical path that led to paradise and serenity. It had now become a memory of my most violent and terrifying experience. It became one more secret that I would store deep down and never tell.

The Long Con

A few weeks had gone by, and I was still feeling a bit jumpy. I continued to go out with my friends but was shying away from meeting new people. I was comfortable going to the ocean and listening to the waves. The salty, clean, fresh air filling my lungs and the warmth of the sand beneath the towel helped me feel grounded and safe. The sound of the waves crashing onto the shore and the call of the gulls lulled me into a calm, relaxed state of mind. One day after spending a long time at the beach, we all had an early dinner, and I decided to stay in. When we got back to the house, I bid everyone good night and headed off to my room. Moments after my head touched the pillow, I drifted off into a deep sleep.

Suddenly, in the middle of the night, I was awakened by my bedroom door crashing open, and in the doorway stood the silhouette of a tall man. My heart began to race; the raw memory of being picked up and carried away filled my mind, and I yelled out to get out of my room.

He stepped into the room towards the bed and responded, "This is my room, who the hell are you?"

Frightened and confused, I switched on the nightstand light and was face-to-face with a stranger. I said, "I am a friend of the owner of the house."

He said, "Well, she is my cousin, and you are in my room."

I argued with him, saying that it had been my room for the summer. I refused to leave the room, and he agreed to sleep on the couch that night but expected me to switch with him in the morning. He turned and walked out, closing the door behind him.

After some time I was able to fall into a light yet guarded sleep. I had been coming here for years with my friends, and this was always my room. I had no idea who this man was or how long he would be staying at the house.

The following morning at breakfast, my friend confirmed that he was in fact her cousin, and he would be staying at the house the remainder of the summer. I was offered the couch in the living room. It was in the middle of the cottage between the kitchen entrance and the bedrooms; there were no doors and no privacy, but it was a place to stay, so I graciously took it.

Early the next morning, around 2:00 a.m., after finally falling into a light, restless sleep, I was awakened by the sound of the front door opening. At that moment, I realized just how exposed I was while sleeping on the couch. I waited quietly in the dark, feeling a sense of panic, then realized it was my friend's cousin.

He came into the room and whispered, "Are you awake?"

Well, I answered irritated, "I am now." I was feeling defensive after our strange introduction the night before.

He came into the den with two cups of coffee in his hands and offered me one. He said, "I want to apologize for the way we had met," and asked if he could sit for a few minutes. He had just gotten off of work as a bouncer and was wide awake. He had the closing shifts at the bar for the summer, and that was why he kept such strange hours.

I accepted his apology and the coffee as he sat on the edge of the couch. Quietly, so as not to wake up anyone else in the cottage, we began having small talk. We talked about school, our majors, and what our goals were after graduation. He seemed like a different person than the intruder I met the night before. After about an hour of chatting, he said good night and thanked me for letting him have his room back. I said no problem; he was after all part of my friend's family; I was simply a guest. I felt lucky to have a place to stay.

For the next few weeks, it became a ritual of shared coffee and hushed whispers at 2:00 a.m. One night, we chatted longer than usual. It was just before dawn, and he asked if I would like to go to the beach and watch the sunrise, so we could continue our conversation and maybe get some breakfast. At this point I was sleep-deprived from the weird hours and quite awake from the coffee, so I agreed.

The sunrise was breathtaking. The sun's rays gently bathed the clouds with gentle pink and salmon colored hues. We sat close together on the hood of the car, silently listening to the crashing waves. The whole experience felt safe and calming to me. We enjoyed a lovely light breakfast and went back to the cottage before anyone woke up. He went to sleep in his room, and I went on the couch. A short time later, my friends and I went back to the beach for another carefree summer day in the sun. I was feeling grateful that I was able to stay on the Cape and enjoy the rest of my school break.

I lay down on the beach; clean, salty ocean air mixed with the distinctive smell of coconut in suntan lotion filled the air. The warmth of the sun on my skin and the rhythmic sound of the ocean all gently lulled me into a sweet slumber. When I awoke, I was feeling refreshed and joyful, thinking about the beautiful sunrise earlier that morning. I began to enjoy our talks and was looking forward to our next early morning encounter.

The next few weeks, we continued our 2:00 a.m. conversations, followed by mornings watching the sunrise before anyone in the house woke up. I was becoming comfortable with him. Our conversations became more intimate, and he encouraged me to share things about me with him. He always listened intently and compassionately. I felt at ease in his company, and I began to share some intimate details of my life. He would sit quietly, nodding, and listening without interruption. The more I shared, the more he seemed to want to know. It was a very intoxicating feeling to have someone pay such close attention to my every word and offer what appeared to me to be such compassion.

One morning he asked if I would stay behind when everyone else went to the beach so we could spend more time together. I thought it sounded nice, as the only time we ever seemed to spend together was in the wee hours of the morning. I told my friends that I was tired and wanted to stay back and get some sleep while the house was quiet.

As we all called out our goodbyes, he came out of his room and sat on the couch with me for a moment. We were alone in the cottage. He didn't say anything; he just leaned in and kissed me for the first time. I felt my heart skip a beat in a moment of panic as I told myself that he was safe. I pushed the memory of the stranger at Duck Pond from my mind.

His kiss was tender and caring, just like our conversations. After a while, he stood up, took my hand, and led me to his room. He gently closed the door, took me in his arms, and walked me over to the bed. He was very tall and had a slender yet muscular build. His shoulders were strong and wide, and his waist was slender. His eyes were the color of a stormy sea, and his dirty blond hair was wild and messy.

I felt my body begin to shake as the memory of the last encounter filled my mind. Once again, I willed myself to store it away. I closed my eyes and forced that memory deep down inside as he ran his hands gently over my body, slowly removing my clothes. His touch calmed me once again. I kept repeating to myself: *This is not the man who raped me; I am safe.* I began to relax as I felt him slowly caressing my body, making me feel a desire I wondered if I would ever feel again. He made love to me with a gentle touch that pushed my level of trust to new heights. I gave myself to him willingly, gratefully, and passionately.

After we made love, as my head was resting on his chest, I felt my fear and terror begin to melt away, tears silently running down my cheeks and dropping onto his naked body. He asked what was wrong, and without lifting my head, I told him I was fine, yet I could not control the release of emotions that I had been holding back. After a few minutes, without lifting my head from his chest, I told him what had happened at Duck Pond.

He was very quiet as I recounted that terrible experience. His breath began to quicken, and I could hear his heart begin to pound. His muscles began to tense as he tightened his hold on me. I just held my breath, feeling fear rise in me again. I was scared and confused. He was the only one I had told since it happened. I felt broken and ashamed.

The tears began to flow more freely, and he held me closer in his arms, and with a deep and menacing tone, he whispered, "Who was it?"

I told him again that I did not know. I had never seen him before and have never seen him since. The tone of his voice became gentle once again, and he lifted my chin to look him in the eye and told me that I was safe now. I believed him.

We continued our late night rendezvous and conversations, and he asked more about my life and experiences. I felt safe for the first time, telling the stories of what had happened to me when I was young and the experiences I had as I was growing up. He listened, as always, intently and with what I thought was compassion and understanding, always ready with a strong shoulder to lean on as I bared my soul to him.

For the rest of the summer, we enjoyed our time together. He began asking where my friends were and where I would be at night. He was becoming very protective. It was comforting in a way to know that someone was watching over me. I felt safe and cared for.

As the summer was coming to an end, we were all preparing to return to our respective schools. Our last day he told me that he had a surprise: he was going to transfer to my school. The university I attended had a more prestigious program in his major than his current school, and he felt it would be the right move for his career as well as be close to me. I was happy that we would not have to say goodbye for the year, and since I lived closer to the school, I offered him a place to stay while he got himself enrolled and comfortable.

He came to my apartment a few days before registration and brought some clothes. We spent the time getting used to a more normal schedule than we had during the summer.

We drove to the university together on the first day of classes. After we got our class schedules and books, we met for lunch. He asked for my schedule to see if we would have any time during the day together. He quickly wrote down my schedule. I thought it was a sweet gesture and felt happy that he was there.

Gradually he moved into my apartment. After a few weeks of him being there, driving to school together, and coming home, we fell into a comfortable routine. The semester passed, the holidays came and went, and before I realized it, he had become my whole world. During the school year, it seemed that the only person I was spending time with was him. He consumed my every waking moment, from driving to classes during the week to spending the weekends together. Somehow, I had lost contact with everyone else.

He slowly became possessive of my time and attention. His behavior began to shift from being protective of me to controlling with a subtle, menacing undertone. The shift in his behavior was so slow that I didn't really notice it was happening. He was critical of my clothes, hair, and demeanor. He began bringing up things that I had shared with him from my past, subtly implying that I was in some way responsible. He no longer made love to me, but rather he became demanding of sex when and how he liked it. I was once again at the will of his desires.

He was only complimentary toward me when I was following his guidelines. I began to dress in a way that would make me unnoticeable to avoid his criticisms. I never wore makeup and always had my hair tied up in a severe bun. It seemed somehow safer not to draw attention to myself.

Summer vacation was upon us once again. We decided to spend the summer on the Cape. He told me that he wanted us to rent our own place for the summer instead of staying with his cousin. All we could afford was a tiny shack, set back from the main road. I remember lying in bed and being able to see the night sky in places through the ceiling. I did my best to make it as cozy as possible; I convinced myself that we would only be sleeping there, so it was not that bad.

He was working nights, so I thought it would give me time to spend with my friends. Happy memories of summers past began to flood into my mind. Partying and dancing to our favorite bands, then heading for the ocean the next day to rest and rejuvenate. I could almost feel the warm sun caressing my skin, taste the clean, salty air on my lips, and hear the rhythmic sound of the waves rolling up on the shore, lulling me into gentle, healing naps on the beach.

When I expressed my excitement about seeing my friends and my plans for what would be our last summer before graduation, he told me that he was uncomfortable with me hanging out with them. My heart sank as I began to feel the anticipation of a last carefree summer slip away before it had a chance to begin. I told him that I felt very strongly about wanting to see my friends and spend time with them, and I watched his blue eyes turn stormy and cold. He seemed to morph before my very eyes into someone I had only had glimpses of. What I had mistaken for a protective nature turned to be completely possessive. I had been submissive to him for so long that he took my words as a challenge that he was not going to tolerate.

The tone of his voice was low and menacing. He walked toward me, and I began to back up until I found myself seated on the couch with him, standing over me. He reminded me that he knew everything about me—all of my darkest secrets, things that I had admitted and confided deep shame and fear of. He began convincing me that I was responsible for what had happened to me when I was young and that night at Duck Pond. He told me that he had information that could hurt not only me but my family and the people I loved. It was at this moment that I realized that all of the nights we had spent talking and confiding, and what I thought was building a friendship and relationship of trust, was him gathering information to use against me.

Instantly I felt as if I were being thrown back into the hall closet with the next door neighbor's hand over my mouth, whispering in my ear threats of revealing secrets. Flashes of being thrown into the back seat of the strange man's car flooded my memory, and I was truly terrified. In my mind, he held total control over me. He had me convinced that if I did not behave the way he thought was proper or acceptable, I would be responsible for my loved ones being harmed. I became, in that moment, his prisoner.

My last summer consisted of staying at the cottage only to leave for the grocery store or if he decided to take me somewhere. When friends stopped by, he would politely tell them that we had plans, and after a while, they just stopped coming. I was permitted to socialize with a select group of people whom he approved of and was instructed to keep quiet about our private lives.

One afternoon we were at a gathering, and a man was talking with me. He said something that made me smile. Later that night, when we got home, I was accused of flirting and being nothing but a whore. He reminded me that I was to behave in such a way as to not bring any attention to myself, or I would be responsible for the fallout that would certainly destroy my family and me. I was shaken to my core. There seemed to be no way out. I had been cut off from my friends and family, but I was responsible for protecting them. I felt myself begin to shut down.

When summer ended, we packed up and moved back to the apartment. One day he came home very excited with the news that he had been accepted to graduate school in California. I felt a sense of relief come over me that he would be so far away. I began to feel hope when he told me that he would do his best to come back as often as possible and had friends that would look out for me when he was gone. That glimmer of hope faded quickly.

The night before his flight out, he presented me with a diamond ring and told me that he wanted me to be his wife. I was in shock as he put the ring on my finger. I felt panic rise in my stomach. All I could think was that I would never be able to escape from this man. I felt as if I were drowning. The next morning I drove him to the airport, and that night I went home to my apartment alone for the first time in over a year.

Upon graduation I was informed that the business my father had been grooming me for was sold to a competitor, and there was a non-nepotism clause. I did not have a position waiting for me any longer. I decided that the only thing to do was to start a business of my own. As I set up my business, I began to feel more confident. The lack of constant stress and judgment from my boyfriend (now fiancé) allowed me to feel a shadow of myself peeking through.

One day, a client requested a night out. He had a reputation for partying hard, and he wanted to go dancing. I had not been dancing in over a year, and it sounded like great fun. I knew that it would be completely unacceptable for me to go alone, so I called a female associate for backup. I thought it would be safe if she was there as a sort of guardian and buffer. She could entertain him on a social level, and I would be safe from any unwanted advances or accusations.

The band was outstanding, and the drinks were strong. Before long, we were all on the dance floor, having a great time. I had not felt that happy and free for what seemed like a lifetime. We closed the bar, and we all went our separate ways. As I came into the apartment, I felt quite wonderful, having been able to entertain a client without breaking any rules for everyone, and I had some harmless fun. Then the phone rang. It was 2:00 a.m.; who could possibly be calling? My heart sank as I thought it must be bad news—no one calls at that hour.

Warily, I lifted the phone off the cradle and said hello. It was my fiancé, and he was furious. He was yelling that he knew where I had been and accused me of being a slut, dancing, and drinking all night. My heart skipped a beat! How could he possibly have known that I was out for the evening? He was in California. My mind raced, I went over the whole evening in a moment and tried to recall if I had done anything wrong. I was only dancing, and I was never once alone on the dance floor without my female associate, but how could he have known any of this? Then it hit me. He had mentioned that he had friends that were going to look out for me. I was being followed and spied on.

I suddenly felt a rage rise up inside of me that made me blind with fury. At that moment, nothing he had threatened me with mattered. I felt the fear leave my soul, and I started yelling back at him. Maybe it was the alcohol that gave me a false sense of security, combined with the fact that he was 3,000 miles away and could not hurt me at the moment, but I let loose on him. I was taking back my power all at once. I told him that it was over. I would send his ring back to him, and he should never contact me again.

As I slammed down the phone, I felt my heart racing and fear flooding my being. I had defied him, and now I would have to suffer the consequences. I was terrified, but there was no going back. I had to stand my ground if I was going to survive.

Over the next few months, he tried to contact me, but I refused to speak with him. When that didn't work, I started getting calls from his family. I refused those calls also. Then letters started arriving in the mail. The first one had no return address, and I made the mistake of opening it. When I saw who it was from, I chose not to read it. I was far too aware of how this man could get into my subconscious and harm me. I simply tore it to pieces and threw it in the trash. Every time I received a letter with no return address, I simply threw it away, unopened.

I was working very hard to find myself again. I felt so broken that I wondered if I would ever fully recover. I was constantly looking over my shoulder, fearful his threats of destruction would come true. They never did. They were empty and designed to control me. I kept a smile on my face and soldiered on silently once again, living with my secrets buried deep down inside. I threw myself into my business, working seven days a week.

The Scorpion and the Frog

During the first year of starting my business, I planned to attend the convention that my father took me to, but on my own. I was looking forward to seeing the Fantasy Man and our annual dance. The dynamics of our relationship had changed as the years passed. I had more life experiences as well as education, and we were now able to talk about business opportunities. I found him to be even more charming than I had fantasized as a young girl. He was from a different part of the country, so we only had contact at this yearly convention or on calls about business opportunities that would benefit either of us in regard to happenings in the industry.

One night before the convention, I got a call from him. He was in Boston on business and invited me to join him for a nightcap at the Ritz Carlton. Images of the fantasy I had created as a young girl came flooding into my memory. I agreed to meet him without a second of hesitation.

I entered the bar and saw him sitting comfortably on a couch in front of a roaring fire. He smiled when he saw me, and I watched as his eyes twinkled in the firelight. He ordered two glasses of port with pears and brie for us to share as we chatted. He sat close to me, and I could feel the warmth of his body almost touching mine. Once again, my mind began wandering to the memories of our many perfect moments on the dance floor. My attention was brought back into the room and the present moment as he began telling me about a potential business opportunity.

I had an early meeting the next day, and it was very late. He waited with me while the valet brought my car around, and I thanked him for the information and a lovely evening. He reached his arm around my waist to open my door, and as I turned to say goodbye, I found myself in his arms. He pulled me closer and kissed me warmly on the mouth.

It was everything I had ever imagined. His lips met mine, and he gently opened my mouth a little with his. His cologne and the sweet smell of his breath filled my senses. My knees went weak for a moment. He said he had wanted to do that for a long time, but he knew my dad and didn't want to be disrespectful to him or to me. I was feeling breathless as I tried desperately to collect my thoughts, searching for a response. I simply smiled, kissed him on the cheek, and thanked him once again for a lovely evening. It took me a few moments to collect myself before driving home.

After that night, our friendship and business relationship continued to grow. Aside from my romantic fantasies, there was never any mention of that one perfect kiss. One day he called about a business opportunity and asked if I would meet him in Miami. He mentioned that it was his birthday and asked if I would join him for dinner after the meeting.

When I made travel arrangements, I decided it would be nice to take a few days and lounge a bit before the meeting. When I arrived at the hotel, I was happy. The grounds were lovely; there was a beautiful pool and not too many guests. The sun was warm and inviting, so I put on my suit and took the time for a quick swim and a cocktail by the pool. The warmth of the sun on my skin, combined with the effect of the cocktail, was very relaxing. The crystal blue sky had just a few wispy clouds. I watched as the rays of the sun sparkled as they reflected off the water in the pool. I was feeling luxuriously pampered.

The meeting went very well. Arrangements were made for future contacts and connections. My friend told me that he would pick me up a few hours later for our dinner. Since we were celebrating his birthday, I wanted to bring him a gift. During our visit to Boston, he mentioned that there was a very rare port that he favored. After a few calls, I was finally able to locate one. It was quite difficult to find, so I carried that bottle on the plane as if it were my child. It never left my possession until I reached the hotel. I was very excited to give him his gift, but decided I would wait until after dinner.

Dinner was delicious, and we were having an easy conversation. As we were waiting for dessert, he looked deeply into my eyes and leaned toward me, taking my hand in his.

He gave me one of his most charming smiles and said to me, "Do you know the story of the Scorpion and the Frog?"

I confessed that I did not, so he proceeded to tell it to me.

"One day there was a scorpion sitting by the edge of a lake. In the lake, there was a frog sitting on a lily pad, enjoying the warmth of the sun. The scorpion asked the frog to please give it a ride across the lake; the frog said, 'No, you will sting me.' The scorpion said, "Now, why would I sting you if I am on your back?' The frog thought about it and agreed to allow the scorpion to climb on his back. Just as they were about to reach the other shore, the scorpion stung the frog. The frog asked why? Why did he do that? The scorpion answered, 'Because I am a scorpion.'"

There was seriousness about the way he was telling me this story. I felt his hand on mine and suddenly realized that in his story, he was warning me that he was the scorpion and I was the frog. I smiled at him very sweetly and with equal seriousness, never releasing him from my gaze. I asked him if he was certain who the scorpion was. He did not answer.

We finished our dessert and headed to my hotel in comfortable silence. When we arrived, I asked him to wait for me in the car; I had a gift for him. I went to my room and retrieved the precious gift I had so carefully picked out for him. The valet was waiting as I presented my fantasy man with this rare treasure. His sincere surprise and appreciation warmed my heart; he assured me that he was aware of how rare this gift was.

He gave me a deep and passionate kiss and whispered, "May I come to your room?"

I could still feel the warmth of his lips on mine as I heard myself say, "No, I have an early flight home." I said, "I look forward to seeing you at the convention." Then I kissed him deeply and wished him a happy birthday. I turned to walk into the lobby and forced myself not to look back.

That year at the cocktail party, the music seemed particularly romantic to me. He came to my table to ask me to dance. As he took my hand in his to lead me onto the dance floor, I felt my entire body flooding with desire for this man. He took me in his arms, my head nestled in his strong shoulder. Once again, the combination of the warmth of his skin and his fragrance filled my senses and my mind. Memories of our last evening together and our passionate kiss goodnight came racing back. It seemed like a dream that I never wanted to end.

After the party, he invited me for a nightcap. We sat in a booth in the lounge of the resort, tucked away in a dark corner. He held my hand gently in his and smiled charmingly as we comfortably shared our drinks. He had a strange effect on me that warmed my heart and created a desire that was almost unbearable.

When we were finished with our drinks, he offered to escort me to my room. Not wanting to miss a moment of this enchanting evening, which I had fantasized about for literally years, I agreed. As we walked silently, hand in hand, down the hall to my door, he turned me to face him and took me in his arms. He lifted my chin up gently and kissed me. I returned his kiss, and I melted into his arms. I felt his body responding to my kiss as he pulled me closer to him.

I suddenly remembered his story about the scorpion and the frog. I decided then and there that I was not going to be the frog. I did not want years of a perfect fantasy to turn into my possible demise. I gently pushed his body away from mine and thanked him for a lovely evening. I opened the door to my room and said good night. As I closed the door behind me, I told myself, sometimes the fantasy is best kept as a fantasy.

Prince Charming

After the long con, I threw myself into work—seven days a week for the next year. I only left my home for work or business functions. While I was waiting for an appointment, I ran into an old high school friend. We chatted as we were waiting for our respective appointments, and he asked me if I was dating anyone. I simply answered no; I was too busy with my business. He told me that he knew a buyer from his industry that he would love to fix me up on a blind date with. I told him I was not interested in being fixed up. He insisted that this buyer was a really nice guy and offered to make it a double date if it would make me feel more comfortable. It had been a very long time since I dated, and I was still quite skittish after my last relationship.

He was very insistent and persuasive, so I agreed to a double date for dinner. My date was quite a few years older than me—well-spoken, polite, and easy to chat with. At the end of the evening, he asked if he could call me, and I agreed. After a few phone calls, we went on another date. He began calling me at the end of each day just to say hello and good night. He treated me kindly and was easy to be with. It seemed as if this could be a safe man to be with. After the last relationship, I wanted to be sure that he was everything he appeared to be.

He treated me to wonderful adventures that included travel to exotic destinations. Every Valentine's Day, a dozen long stem red roses and a box of Godiva chocolate truffles were delivered to me. Each year we met in Manhattan. Our evening's adventure began with a bottle of Dom Perignon chilling as a stretch limousine waited to take us to and from the theater. He had 7th row center seats to Broadway shows, followed by dining at exclusive five-star restaurants. I felt like I was living in a dream. We dated for several years, and I was sure he was the real thing. I thought I had found my prince charming.

During a cruise to South America, on the top deck, under a full moon, he asked me to do him the honor of becoming his wife. It felt surreal. I had no idea he was going to propose, and I said, "Yes!" He slipped a sparkling, two-carat princess-cut diamond on my finger.

We chose a date a few weeks after our engagement and wedding plans began. One day he called in the middle of the day and sounded very upset; he told me he had just been laid off. It happened so suddenly that he was blindsided and didn't know what to do.

He said, "Maybe we should call off the wedding."

I told him that was not the answer and asked him if there was any job he would want to do. What would it be?

"I want to do what you do," he answered.

For the past fifteen years, he had been a senior buyer at a world known firm, and I was a manufacturer's representative. He wanted to jump from being a buyer to a salesman? I told him that he would have some major adjustments to make. He was used to making all the decisions and having all the power on a sales call. Essentially, he was the boss. People don't understand that when you work for yourself, especially in sales, everyone becomes your boss—not only the buyer, but the companies you represent.

He was in NYC at his industry convention at the time, so I advised him to contact his largest manufacturer (the people he had been generous to over the years in purchasing) and let them know he intended to start a sales firm and wanted to represent them. I met him in Manhattan that evening and spent the rest of the week with him, mapping out a plan to meet with potential clients and begin his new journey on the other side of the desk.

He had a successful week securing work, and we made arrangements for him to set up an office and print business cards. He was a natural, and his business was up and running in no time. He was very busy with his new business that he left the wedding arrangements up to me.

My dream was to have a small intimate wedding, be taken to a church in a horse-drawn carriage, and then have dinner at my favorite Italian restaurant. Unfortunately, this was not to be. My wedding became a double-industry gala event. We both worked in the same market, but in different categories. When people heard about the wedding, they began inviting themselves. Before I knew it, my intimate wedding had a guest list of 575 people. I had to reserve three ballrooms in the local hotel to accommodate that many people.

My dad was part owner of an Italian bakery and took it upon himself to gift us with a beautiful assortment of pastries as well as my cake. He insisted on surprising me with the cake, and I saw it for the first time as I entered the reception hall. This cake was spectacular! It had three tiers (not layers, but tiers) and three sections connected by small bridges, mini waterfalls, and elegant twinkling lights.

When the band plugged in their sound equipment in combination with this opulent cake, the fuses in all three ballrooms blew. We were plunged into darkness. In a panic, the band leader came to me and apologized. I just laughed lightly and replied, "I think it's the cake that overloaded the fuses. We can unplug the cake while you are playing." He smiled and thanked me for being understanding.

The music began, and I was whisked onto the dance floor by relatives and guests. I was given a small satin pouch to carry on my wrist, and soon I began to feel like my wedding looked like a scene from The Godfather. Well-wishing guests, some of whom I had never met, greeted me respectfully with congratulations and handed me envelopes to place in my pouch.

We danced the night away and were the last to leave the party. Since quite a few of our guests were from out of town, we hosted a morning brunch and then left for our honeymoon that afternoon. My husband and I had purchased a condo near the beach; he suggested we spend our honeymoon there to save money. I was a little disappointed that instead of relaxing and enjoying our honeymoon, I would be required to cook, clean, and do laundry, but I understood. He was building a new business, and the beach was beautiful.

On the third day of our honeymoon, we sat on the beach, enjoying a picnic lunch that I had prepared. My new husband informed me that he wanted to get back to work. He wanted to leave that afternoon to start early the next day. I could barely believe what I was hearing. I had cleared my calendar for a week to have a chance to relax after planning the extravagant event our wedding had turned into. I was looking forward to enjoying our time alone as newlyweds. My heart was heavy as I realized I was being left on a beach halfway through my honeymoon. This was not the romantic man I had been dating for seven years. I was confused and hurt. I was not ready to leave. I had just spent months planning this wedding by myself, and I was determined to enjoy my time away.

We had taken separate cars as we were bringing things for the condo. I told him that if he wanted to, he should go, but I was going to remain here for the rest of my time since I had taken off from work and would see him when I got back. We left the beach, and he got in his car and drove away. As I watched him drive out of the parking lot, I wondered who this stranger was. I was feeling confused and sad. This was not what I had thought my wedding or honeymoon would look like. I began to wonder what the rest of my life was going to look like if this was how it was starting.

I took the next few days to relax, walk on the beach, lie in the sun, and treat myself to a few dinners out. I convinced myself that his odd behavior was just the stress of starting a new business, and I could understand that.

The following month was my industry's yearly convention. I explained to my husband that this was the event where manufacturers interviewed potential businesses to represent them. It was agreed that my husband could come, but he would have to find his own entertainment during the day. Nighttime was for dinners and parties. He spent a week lounging by the pool, playing golf, relaxing, and enjoying the resort while I was attending back-to-back meetings, working to build my business and add new products to my mix. Representatives were there from all over the country. Competitors as well as old friends heartily greeted each other, passing in the lobby in between appointments. My husband and I saw each other at dinners, and then I was off early in the morning to meetings and presentations.

The last night of the convention was the big event, the semi-formal cocktail party. It had always been my favorite event. I was looking forward to dancing to the sounds of romantic music with my new husband.

I had already made a salon appointment to have my hair blow-dried straight. My thick, frizzy hair reached the top of my hips, and that did not play well with the moisture of the semi-tropical humidity. As a general rule, either I had it tied up in a secure bun with a lot of gel, or on cool, dry days, I would go to the hairdresser to have it professionally blown straight. I knew this would be at least a two-hour process, so I booked my appointment early enough that I would not have to rush to get dressed.

We were staying in a very exclusive resort, and the hair salon was up-to-date on all the newest trends. I knew from experience that my hair had a mind of its own. The only way to control it was to have it done by a professional. When I told the stylist what I wanted, he asked if he could try something different. If I hated it, he would then do as I requested. He assured me that no scissors were involved, and he would have plenty of time to fix it if need be.

He spun me away from the mirror, so I could not see what he was doing. He took special care, using products that, he said, "were new to the market and developed especially for my type of hair." When he finished, he turned me towards the mirror, and all I could see were curls. Not frizz, just shiny, black spiral curls that draped elegantly over my shoulders and down to my waist.

He laughed when he saw my face and said, "You had no idea you had these curls, did you?" I just shook my head, a little stunned and speechless at how beautiful my curls were. The only way I had ever attempted to wear my hair was tied up tight and controlled, or perfectly straight. It was the first time my hair felt free—not a tangled, frizzy mess, tamed only by being pulled straight with a hot iron, but a riot of glorious curls.

I was so excited to go back to the room to show my new husband my beautiful new hairstyle. I walked into the room and asked him what he thought, expecting him to see my joy and hoping he loved it as well. Instead his response was rather cold. He looked at me and said, "You paid for that?" I was crushed. I nearly burst into tears. What if it was horrible, and I was just fooling myself into thinking that I looked pretty?

I began to feel insecure as I put on the beautiful dress I had chosen for the event and questioned whether I could really pull this wild and free hairstyle off. It was too late to change my mind, so I put on my make-up and, with a brave smile, walked in silence with my husband to the ballroom.

As we slowly made our way to the event, I was greeted with a few long looks, then sudden recognition, and to my delight, the response of, "Oh my goodness, I almost didn't recognize you. Your hair is amazing!" I was a little wary since I got such a strange, negative response from my husband. The more positive reactions I received reinforced my original feelings about my hair. I decided to embrace my beautiful, new hair style and the evening. It had been a long week of meetings and work, and I was determined to enjoy myself.

When we walked into the ballroom, the lilting sounds of the band playing soft, romantic music filled the air. I asked my husband if he would like to dance, and he said, "No." I was really not sure what had put him in such an unpleasant mood; I sat down at the table with him once again, feeling disappointed. I looked up, and I saw my fantasy man smile as he approached me to ask for our annual dance. I felt my heart flutter for a moment as memories of years past raced through my mind. I gratefully accepted his hand, and he led me onto the floor.

With the natural grace that this man possessed, he twirled me to face him, took me gently in his arms as he had for years, and whispered in my ear how lovely I looked that evening. He complimented my new hairstyle, told me that it was very attractive, and assured me that I wore it beautifully. I felt as if I had finally made it to the ball as he led me around the dance floor, cradled securely in his arms. The room seemed to disappear for a moment, and all I could hear was the beautiful music. Once again, I could see no one but him. Charming as always, he put me at ease as I felt myself melting into his familiar embrace. He was a perfect gentleman; he walked me back to my table and my husband.

An announcement was made that there was a photographer in the outer area who was taking portraits for those who were interested. Quickly, a line of women dressed in their beautiful cocktail dresses and men in their suits were lining up for their memento of the evening. I am generally extremely camera shy, but that evening I was feeling so beautiful in my new dress and my fun new hair style that I asked my husband if he would please come with me to take a picture. He flat out refused, telling me to go ahead if I wanted to.

Determined not to let my husband ruin my evening, I decided I would go myself. I joined the line of couples, and as I was waiting my turn, my fantasy man walked by and asked, "Why are you alone?" I told him honestly that my husband was not interested in having his picture taken. He stepped right in line beside me and told me he would be honored to have a picture taken with me. I honestly didn't think twice about it. We had been friends for years, and I was happy not to be standing alone in a line of couples.

The evening continued, a little uncomfortably due to my husband's dark mood. I did my best to socialize one last time, making sure I said hello to all the people I had met with and thanked them once again for their time and attention during the week. At the end of the evening, my husband and I walked up to the room in silence. I asked him what was going on, and he just said "nothing."

The next morning, we had an early flight, as did most of the people at the event. We all had our luggage in the lobby, waiting for our transportation to the airport as we said our final farewells. One man in particular, a loud Texan, whose business I had been vying for, came to say goodbye and let me know that he was considering my firm to represent him. I was ecstatic. This would be a million dollar account. I told him how pleased I was, and he slipped his arm around my waist to give me a hug. He wasn't being inappropriate; he was just a boisterous physical person. Suddenly, out of nowhere, my husband came storming up behind me and said loud enough for any bystanders to hear, "You are a married old hag now; it's about time you started acting like it, not a whore."

You could suddenly hear a pin drop. The manufacturer took his arm away, and I watched his face drop. He said he was very sorry if there was a misunderstanding. I was mortified, bright red with embarrassment. I assured him that he had nothing to apologize for. I thanked him for the opportunity, knowing full well that I had just lost the line.

I turned and looked at my new husband with fury in my eyes. I walked directly toward him and, in a low, growling tone, told him to get the bags; we would wait outside. He followed me and tried to talk, and I just shook my head. I had nothing to say to him. By the time we returned home from the convention, I had once again convinced myself that his behavior was due to the stress of starting a new business. I was determined to become the partner he needed in our marriage and to help him with his new career. He worked very hard to build his business as I continued to grow my own.

We began to travel to our condo separately due to conflicting schedules, and I was quite comfortable with the occasional solitude of my mini retreats. The more time I spent alone, the more aware I became of our differences in beliefs and values. I wondered how these things had never been apparent during our seven years of dating.

We had very different ideas of what marriage and our respective roles as husband and wife should be. Slowly, he became more demanding and critical of the things that I did and said. After a number of years, I began to realize that we were not communicating at all. Simple conversations became arguments, and he began raising his voice to me.

I suggested that we see a marriage counselor, but he was resistant, telling me our business was our own. I was determined to do everything I could to save our marriage, but I simply could not live in the atmosphere that we had created. One evening, after a particularly brutal verbal confrontation, I said, "Either we find a marriage counselor to help us learn to communicate, or this is over." Under duress, he agreed but left it up to me to do the research.

I finally found a marriage counselor, under his insistence, who was a male. I made our first appointment. He seemed fair and listened intently to both of our descriptions of what we thought was happening in our marriage. After all, there are always two sides to every story.

My main complaint was that my husband did not listen to me or seem to care about my feelings. He said he didn't see that we had any problems and felt it was all in my mind. The counselor suggested we come back the following week and gave us some homework to do and to assist in communication skills. We rode home together in silence.

During the week I attempted to work with him on some of the suggestions, but he simply shut me out. He had stopped yelling and arguing with me, but now he wasn't speaking to me at all. He would turn on the television and flip through channels, choosing whatever show interested him, and there we sat together, miles apart.

One night, he was watching a crime show that contained a violent rape scene. I felt myself freeze, and I became quite emotional. I begged him to please turn off the station, and he laughed at me and refused, saying that it would be over in a minute. I would have left the room during it, but I felt paralyzed. Memories flood my mind of the closet door closing behind me, being thrown into the back seat of the strangers' car at Duck Pond, and the long con's words ringing in my ears that people I love would be harmed if I didn't do exactly as I was told.

I realized that over the last seven years, I had told him very little about what had happened to me in the past. It had been used against me so many times that I had stuffed it deep inside of me and locked the door. Part of me believed that as long as I didn't speak of it, it would be as if it never happened.

During the next counseling session, I began to open up about some of my experiences and commented about how unsafe I felt during that scene in the movie. His reaction to my request to change the channel was alarming to me, though I gave him the benefit of the doubt, realizing that he did not have the information about my personal experience. He restated that it didn't seem like I should make such a big deal over it.

Seeing that I was clearly affected by this turn of events, as well as my beginning to open up, even a little, about what I had personally experienced, the counselor gave my husband some books to look over in regard to helping a loved one who had been abused. He took the books, and we left once again, riding home in silence.

When we got home, he threw the books on the table, and, there, they remained untouched for the entire week. He continued to give me the silent treatment night after night, and if I attempted to ask if he had looked over any of the books, he would just turn his back to me and walk away. I was beginning to feel a deep sense of hopelessness.

The following week, I shared what was happening with the counselor. He turned his attention to my husband to ask his opinion. My husband just shook his head disinterestedly as if he had not even heard a word of what I said. I said, "Now do you see what I mean when I say that I don't feel like he listens?"

The counselor then asked him why he thought we were seeing him.

His answer was, "I'm here just waiting for her to get better."

This answer seemed to take the counselor aback for a moment, and he said, "No, we are here to help you learn how to communicate in your marriage."

This infuriated my husband, and he made it clear that it would be the last time he would come to these sessions. At his remark, the counselor looked at me and said, "Honestly, the two of you are like oil and water. I don't see how you ever got together in the first place."

I made the decision after that session that I would contact a divorce lawyer. I told him that I was going to do this and suggested he do the same. Months passed, and he continued to ignore me. When he did speak to me, he was clearly annoyed and bordering on angry, until one day he blew up at me over a simple question. I felt my blood run cold as memories of being abused came rushing back to me.

The next morning I called my lawyer and told him I no longer felt safe in my home. The lawyer asked what time my husband would be home and told me that he would send a sheriff over to serve him with a restraining order. My heart was pounding. I had never taken a stand for myself like this before, and I was feeling frightened. After dinner there was a knock on the door, and I asked my husband to answer the door.

To his surprise there was an officer asking my husband to identify himself. When he did, the sheriff presented restraining papers and told him he had to leave the premises. He could gather some belongings until arrangements were made for him to return for the rest of his things.

I was standing at the top of the stairs, the officer waiting at the door, as my husband turned and looked at me and said, "Are you serious?"

I responded that I had been telling him for months to contact a lawyer. He just said to me that I should prepare myself for the longest, ugliest divorce in history. He gathered a few things and was escorted out. He was true to his word; the divorce took five years, and I was left with not much more than the house with a mortgage.

Sifu

At some point, time began to bend for me—relationships from the past began to come back and fold into the present. Little did I know that the day I found an ad in the paper for an introductory Tai Chi would become one of those turning points.

I was looking for something that would get me moving and help me channel my energy in a healthy and positive way. I came across an advertisement for Tai Chi classes. The ad described the class as "moving meditation." I gave them a call and went that evening for an introductory class.

When I arrived there was a class in progress; I stopped to watch through the observation window. The instructor was demonstrating a form for the class. His movements were fluid and powerful. His energy was controlled, focused, and intense. I admired his flexibility, strength, and endurance. I could almost feel his every move in my own body. He had a raw sexual energy that held my undivided attention.

I barely heard my name as I was greeted by the person I had spoken with on the phone. He introduced himself as *Sifu* (teacher) and explained that what I was watching was the Kung Fu class. He told me that the Tai Chi class he taught was much slower and gentler than what I had just witnessed. I felt relieved as I was looking for something more meditative as the ad had stated.

Sifu invited me to stay for the Tai Chi class that was scheduled in a few minutes. The class involved stretching and a slow introduction to various individual postures. At the end, Sifu demonstrated the full form that the class was learning. He cued up soft music that set the pace as he gracefully and skillfully moved from one posture to the next. I watched his movements flowing, almost seamlessly from one posture to the next, and I felt my body gently swaying along. It truly appeared to be a moving meditation. This was the class I had been looking for.

Every now and then, I would show up early to watch the Kung Fu class that was held before ours. I was able to watch through the observation window into the classroom without being noticed. The Kung Fu sifu continued to hold my fascination from afar. He had personal power that was palpable and breathtaking. I was particularly fascinated when he did sword form. The swords became an extension of his body, moving through the air with effortless power.

After a few months of classes, we were informed that the school was closing down, but the Tai Chi classes would still be taught at a gym near my house. It was actually more convenient for me. There was a core group of students who were very dedicated. We began to bond over shared dinners after class and occasionally gather at Sifu's apartment to watch movies and have impromptu lessons. I was the only woman in the group. My fellow students and Sifu became like brothers to me.

After some time, the classes stopped being held at the gym and were being held in Sifu's yard. He lived very close by, and I would occasionally go over a little early to visit. He was easy to be with, and I enjoyed his company. We began spending more time alone, going for walks, and spontaneously practicing form together. I was incredibly comfortable with him as he slowly became a friend and confidant.

One day, he shared with me that it was his dream to go to Colorado. He wanted to buy a yurt (a portable round tent), and live off the land. There was no question in my mind that he would be perfectly suited for that lifestyle. He was happiest when he was outdoors, climbing mountains and hiking in the woods. He was content with minimal necessities. I had never met anyone like him and thought he was quite interesting. I loved listening to his dreams and plans for the future. We came from very different worlds. I could not imagine the lifestyle he was describing, but I enjoyed watching as his eyes would light up when he talked about it.

One night he told me that he was ready to go. His plan was to leave by the end of the month, and though I felt sad that he would be leaving and very sad that class would be ending, I was happy for him. Then, to my surprise, he told me that he wanted me to go with him. I burst out laughing. Surely he was joking. I said that would never work for me. I like the convenience of indoor plumbing and electricity. I would simply not survive without my hairdryer.

We had become close friends, and I told him I would be truly heartbroken if I never heard from him again. He promised to keep in touch. The night before he was scheduled to leave for his new life, he called and asked if he could come and visit with me to say goodbye. When he came over, we decided to watch a movie.

We settled in on the couch as we had done many times before, snuggled up close to each other. I felt him place his hand on my thigh and felt a rush of excitement run through my body. He had never touched me intimately before. I turned to face him, and he kissed me. What began as a gentle kiss on the lips quickly became deep and intense.

I could feel my breath quickening and my body responding to his kiss. He gently pressed me against the couch and began unbuttoning my shirt. I did not object. I felt comfortable, and his touch felt familiar as if he had touched me a thousand times before. Neither one of us spoke. I felt like we were in a slow motion movie.

He positioned me so I was reclining comfortably against a pillow and leaned over me, grasping the arms of the couch behind me. He didn't say a word and, without once breaking eye contact with me, entered into me. His movements were slow and deliberate. I responded to his touch, my body moving towards him, wanting him to be as deep inside of me as possible. Matching the rhythm of my movements, he started to move faster and harder until I felt myself suddenly climaxing as we came together.

Breathless, we lay in each other's arms. We didn't speak for quite a while; we just held each other without moving. He asked if I was ok, and I answered yes. We didn't talk about what happened. We got dressed, and he said that he had to go, or he would never leave me. I was speechless. I walked him to the door and hugged him as we said goodbye. He promised he would call me when he got to Colorado and kissed me good bye. I watched him walk away without looking back.

A few days passed before he called to let me know that he had arrived safely. I had thought long and hard about our last night together and came to the decision that, although the sudden passion between us was intense and wonderful, we were much better off as friends. We could never be more than that.

Over the next ten years, we remained best friends and occasionally spontaneous lovers. Although these times were always intense and passionate, they never seemed to affect our deep friendship. When we were in relationships with other people, there was no jealousy. We supported each other with a sweet confidence that we always had someone safe to confide in. He was the first person I ever felt loved me, unconditionally, and I him.

Every once in a while, in between relationships, he would ask," Why don't you just come and be with me?" I would always respond lightly, thinking he was surely joking. I loved him deeply and dearly, but there was simply no way we would ever be happy together. We were just too different, not only in lifestyle, but basic needs and desires. No, this was never an option. He never seemed upset by my rejections; it seemed to me that it was something he would say to cheer me up. His consistent unconditional love was one of the most cherished gifts I had ever received.

Teacher

A few months after Sifu left, I was looking for another place to study Tai Chi when I came upon a flyer for a local workshop. I signed up, and that is when I met Teacher. I enjoyed the pace of the class as well as the wealth of information he had to share. After class, he was sitting alone at the registration desk. I approached the desk to thank him for the class and ask if he taught any weekly classes. Without raising his eyes, he simply said no. I wasn't sure if he said no, just to me, or no, he did not have weekly classes. So I asked how I would find information on his next seminar. I was determined to study with him, one way or another.

    He sighed and finally looked up at me. He asked me why I wanted to study with him, and I told him that I enjoyed his style of teaching and that I would love the opportunity to learn more. He invited me to come to a regular class, but he warned me that he did not have a traditional school. He gave me an address as well as the days and times they met.

The classes were very informal; they were held outside, with no curriculum, just practice, in random places, and in all kinds of weather. We practiced in sweltering heat, rain, snow, and even ice storms. The only time class was cancelled was if it was windy. We practiced in parking lots and in parks. Classes were held three days a week, and we were invited but not required to attend. I made it a habit to never miss a class. I was the only woman in the company of six to eight other men including the Teacher. Most of them were black belts in various styles of martial arts. I was just a beginner, but I was dedicated to the practice and teachings.

He rarely gave verbal instructions. At the beginning of each class, he would demonstrate a posture or two, and we were to do our best to replicate his movements. As we practiced he would go around the class silently and adjust our stance and structure. His movements were sometimes so subtle you could barely detect them, yet they were the essence of smooth transitions in forms. These transitions and postures, when combined, became a beautiful moving meditation.

At the end of each class, one student was chosen by the teacher to walk with him, giving them the opportunity to ask questions. I watched as the others vied for his attention while I kept quiet and did my best to be invisible in the background. I felt like I was back in grade school, praying the teacher did not call on me. I didn't have a clue as to where to begin with a one-on-one conversation with him.

One day in early autumn, he singled me out to take a walk. I had no idea what I was supposed to ask. Everything was still so new to me. My heart skipped a beat as he told me to follow him. We walked together for a while in silence. The air was cool and crisp. I watched as the sky began to turn beautiful shades of orange, pink, and purple with the setting sun.

He headed towards a path leading into a wooded area. I followed respectfully as we continued our silent stroll, hyper-focused on his every movement. He stopped, sat down on a fallen log, and invited me to join him. I was feeling vulnerable, but safe alone with him.

As he began to speak, I noticed his voice was deep, warm, and inviting. Listening to him speak had a calming effect on me. I heard him say that he spoke five languages and asked me how many I spoke. This brought me out of the light trance I seemed to have fallen into. I laughed a little nervously, answering, just one, and sometimes poorly. I was becoming quite fascinated by this man. He appeared to be wonderfully calm and grounded. These qualities were very attractive to me.

He just smiled and asked about me. I told him that I had just been through a messy, unpleasant divorce. He listened with empathy and attentiveness. He was eight years older than me and appeared to have a certain mature wisdom and understanding that made me feel quite at ease. He thanked me for walking with him and sharing my story.

We stood and continued our walk in silence. He escorted me to my car, and I thanked him for the one-on-one time and told him I appreciated his time. I felt comfortable in his presence. As I was about to leave, he stopped me and said that he was teaching a beginner's intensive workshop that weekend, and he asked me to help him with the class. He needed someone to register the students, take their payments, and assist some of the students during the seminar. He told me that he noticed how closely I paid attention to his instructions and felt that I would be able to help with any new students.

I registered each student and assigned them a group number. Each group had six students. As each posture or movement was demonstrated by the Teacher, I would assist him by watching the students and helping them if they had any questions. This way he could be sure that each group had personal attention, and any corrections or questions that I could not make or were unsure of could be addressed by him after each segment.

I was surprised by how many questions I knew the answers to without having to check with Teacher. Any self-doubt I had soon subsided, and I relaxed into the role of teacher's assistant. The students did a wonderful job, and the day was declared a success with promises of a follow-up workshop in a few months.

As Teacher and I said our goodbyes to the students, we started packing up to go. Feeling exhilarated from the energy of the day and the success of the workshop, we left for the parking lot. As we started to walk around the building, he turned toward me, easily lifted me off the ground, and carried me a few steps backward, gently pressing me up against the cool bricks. Before I could say a word, he kissed me gently and fully on the lips. This spontaneous act of passion was thrilling and had a romantic air about it.

He placed me back on the ground and told me he wanted to do that for a long time. It had been a long time since I had been kissed like that. I liked it and missed it. My body felt as if it were waking from a long sleep. I was so surprised by his kiss and my reaction; I didn't know what to say. I just looked at him and smiled a little. He walked me to my car, thanked me for my help, and told me he would see me in class.

The next night at class, everything was completely normal. Teacher briefly mentioned the success of the workshop and gave me a mention for a job well done. It seemed that I was the only one he invited to assist him. I watched as a light shadow of envy passed over the faces of the other students. I made note of this and decided not to talk about any of the events that occurred to anyone and simply say it was a success.

After class Teacher asked me to stay, saying he would like a word with me. I remained; my heart was pounding, my mind was reeling, and my body was tingling with the memory of his lips pressing upon mine as he held me up against the cool bricks of the building. I thought we would have a private moment to talk about what happened. He did not mention the day before, but asked if I would assist him with a project he was working on. I told myself, the kiss was just the excitement of the day for him and tried to put it out of my mind.

He was writing an instruction manual for one of the forms he was teaching and needed assistance. I agreed to help, and we set a time to meet at his apartment the next day. When I arrived, there were loose pages of work strewn about the living room floor. He told me that the manual would have diagrams of the postures. I was given the task of labeling his diagrams as well as putting them in the correct sequences.

While I was working on the pictorial sequences, he continued to write the corresponding text. We worked in silence for a few hours before it was time to break for lunch and relax for a bit. As we sat at the table and chatted about his book, we discussed various options for printing and distribution when the book was complete.

He reached over to me and took my hand gently. He looked into my eyes and smiled. He thanked me for taking the time to work with him and asked if I would accept an offer of free classes as payment for my work. I told him that would be perfectly acceptable, and we agreed to a weekly schedule that coincided with our classes.

A few weeks passed by quickly. We met three times each week. I arrived at noon, and we worked until class began. At 5:30, we stopped to change into our workout clothes and walk down to the designated area before any other students arrived. He told me that the manual was going to be a surprise release and asked me to please not mention our work to anyone in the class. Happy to be a part of his plan, I agreed to keep it a secret until the great reveal. We never mentioned our time together; I made it a habit of putting my daytime clothes into the car before class, so no one would question why I had a second set of clothes. It was all very clandestine, and it was more than a little exciting to be a part of the surprise.

After the first month of our weekly work sessions, we had made great progress toward the completion of his book. When I arrived that day, Teacher told me how much he appreciated me keeping my word and not telling anyone what we were up to. What he did not know was that I was a "keeper of secrets," and this one was easy. It was quite exhilarating to be a part of his creation and get to know him on a more personal level. He spoke about living in Israel and his travels to China, learning various forms from his teachers in their native languages.

One day as we were standing at the door to leave for class, he placed his hands on my shoulders, slid his right hand up the back of my neck to my hairline, and simultaneously moved his left hand to the center of my back, effortlessly turning my body towards him as he gathered a handful of my hair, close to my scalp, and ever so gently tightened his hold as he leaned my head back, slightly lifting my face towards his. He did not say anything; he just leaned down and kissed me, this time deeply and passionately. I felt a surge of energy run through my body. He released his hold on me without saying a word, opened the door, and we walked down to class.

One of the students had come early and, as we walked up, commented that my face was all red. My mind was racing; Teacher just looked at me and said, "Yes, it is," with a small grin. I just shook my head a little and walked away. I was still tingling with the excitement from feeling of his hands in my hair and on my back. I had his scent in my nostrils and the lingering sensation of his kiss on my lips.

As class began, Teacher announced that we would be doing an exercise called "sticky or sensing hands" to improve our awareness of our balance as well as our partners. He wanted us to increase our sense of awareness of subtle energies. Through slow and gentle flowing movement with just our wrists, forearms, and hands, we were able to sense where our opponent was vulnerable and, at that moment, apply a small amount of pressure to push them off balance.

My body felt like a live wire. My skin was sensitive to the air around me, and my nostrils were still filled with his clean, woodsy smell. I took a deep breath, and, as I exhaled, I allowed myself to settle into a strong stance.

I placed my wrists against my partners, and we waited for the signal to begin the "sensing hands" exercise. I slid my hands along his arms to his elbows, feeling his structure and balance—no weaknesses. I continued to move my hands up his arms and to his shoulders, searching for the weakness, and then down the front of his chest. As I came to his abdomen, I turned my body slightly to guide my hand close to, but not touching his upper groin. I felt him twitch slightly, and I gently applied some pressure. His hip folded, and he toppled gently to the ground.

I offered him a hand as he commented that doing this exercise with me was like being made love to. Overhearing this comment, Teacher started to laugh, and I turned bright red. My partner quickly apologized, saying that he meant no disrespect to me, only that my touch was much different than practicing with the men. He continued to explain himself by saying that my touch was gentle and fluid, and he noticed that I never broke contact with him from the moment we began until he was on the ground. Teacher commented, "Well, that is quite a compliment."

During this exercise, each student had the opportunity to work with Teacher; he never spoke, just moved. I was last in line for the evening. Everyone was partnered up and very focused on each other. I lifted my arms and offered them to Teacher. For a moment, I felt as if I was offering myself to him. My energy was vibrating out of control being that close to him. He looked deeply into my eyes and seemed to lock me in a trance.

My first partner's comment, "Doing this exercise with you is like making love" was still ringing in my ears. The warmth of the teacher's hands and his slow, deliberate gestures, tracing my body, began to excite me. Thoughts of what it would be like to feel his skin on mine filled my mind. I felt his hand on my stomach, and, as I felt it flutter from his touch, he applied just enough pressure to let me know I was off balance. He caught me, and we continued the game until the end of class. During those few minutes, it seemed as if the class had disappeared, and we were engaged in a slow and seductive dance. We moved together in perfect harmony. It was thrilling and seamless. I closed my eyes and allowed my other senses to take over just for a moment, and it felt as if we were one. Suddenly I felt myself being gently pushed, and it brought me back to reality. He caught me once again; he gently steadied me on my feet and announced class was over.

Everyone said their goodbyes, got into our cars, and went our separate ways. My mind was racing, my muscles were sore from the workout, and my body was on fire. The secrecy of all of it was both intriguing and wildly exciting. I felt as if we had somehow slipped into a secret romantic relationship.

I lay awake that night, imagining how it might feel to let go of the feeling that I had to be in control. My ex-husband had become very critical and controlling during our marriage. I was tired of fighting, and tired of being told I was not behaving properly, tired of having to feel like I had to watch every word and movement I made. I had been alone for years after my marriage ended. I had become guarded and untrusting. The only man who was able to break through momentarily was Sifu.

Teacher was awakening parts of me that I had convinced myself no longer existed. I began to feel alive, excited, and sensual. His energy was quietly powerful and seductive. When I went to work the next day, I had a feeling of adventure and curiosity. He greeted me at the door and invited me to sit and talk for a bit.

He told me that he was having strong feelings for me and would like very much to explore them deeper, but he wanted to keep them between us. He did not want our relationship to interfere with the dynamics of the class. It had taken me some time to be accepted as the only woman in the group. I certainly didn't want to be judged or perceived as anything but the hard working fellow student that I was. I did not need anyone to know that we had a relationship outside of class. We agreed that our relationship outside of class would remain just between us.

He was worldly and knowledgeable, nearly a decade my senior. I found him quite interesting. Slowly I began to drop my guard. He told me that he would like to share some experiences with me. He would let me know how, and he would assure me that I would always have full control. I had no idea what he had in mind, but I was intrigued.

One day when I arrived ready to begin work for the day, he informed me that we would be doing an exercise to heighten my awareness by engaging in a little sensory deprivation.

His plan was to work with my olfactory system and my sense of taste. He would first hold something beneath my nose for me to identify, and then he would offer it to me to eat. I was instructed to eat whatever he placed in my mouth slowly and mindfully. He assured me that I would be safe. He would not do anything that was not designed for my pleasure. I agreed, and he asked if he could blindfold me. As he placed a black sash over my eyes, I was plunged into total darkness. I closed my eyes beneath the blindfold and controlled my breathing, attempting to relax as I waited for his instructions.

I sat comfortably on the couch in the darkness as I listened to him move about the kitchen. I listened as cabinets and drawers opened and closed, then the refrigerator door. I heard the quick, sharp sound of a knife against a wooden cutting board. A few minutes later, he came back into the room. He asked if I was comfortable, and I replied yes. My thoughts were spinning, and my senses began to reel as he lifted his first offering under my nose. It was a strawberry; it smelled fresh and clean. The freshly sliced flesh of the fruit released a sweet fragrance that I could almost taste. He told me to open my mouth, and he carefully placed the delicious fruit on my tongue. I held it in my mouth for a moment, savoring the sweet, firm flesh, then chewed it slowly, releasing a burst of flavor that filled my senses.

Next, he offered me a piece of fresh pineapple. The tropical fragrance was sweet and acidic. As he placed it in my mouth, I felt the sweet juices run down my throat. Images of relaxing on a beach filled my mind. I took a deep breath and felt my body begin to relax as I imagined the warm sun caressing my skin.

Saving the best for last, he held up a dark chocolate truffle. After the intense, fresh essence of the fruit, the subtle smell of cocoa tickled my nose. I identified it as chocolate; it seemed to have subtle notes and layers of intensity. As he cut the truffle in half, the smell of the dark chocolate exploded in my nostrils. My mouth immediately began to water. I opened my mouth and waited for him to place it gently on my tongue. He told me to just allow it to melt in my mouth and savor each moment. As the truffle rested on my tongue, it released intense layers of sweetness, with notes of coffee and cocoa combined to create the perfect treat.

I felt him lean towards me; my nostrils were filled with the light clover scent of his soap and the warmth of his breath. He stopped just before placing his lips against mine, and I could feel the energy between us—that sweet feeling of electricity that happens just before you kiss. My breath began to quicken, and I could feel my body responding in anticipation of his touch just before our lips met.

He kissed me slowly and passionately, and in that moment, his warm, sweet kiss became indistinguishable from the perfect treats placed in my mouth. As he pulled away, he released the sash from my eyes. I looked up at him with a look of pure desire. He was pleased by my response, smiled knowingly, and left me sitting there for a moment, basking in the sensory adventure I had just been given.

Before we left for class that evening, he told me that he was going to put a message on his answering machine that would be meant for me. He warned that to anyone else, it would sound generic, but I should know it was intended for me to hear. His voice was deep and sultry, and I was already wondering what he would say. He had spent the morning, playing with my sense of smell, taste, and feeling of his lips on mine; now he was planning on filling my mind through the sound of his voice and his words designed as a secret message of seduction. It was all I could do to concentrate in class.

The following week, when I arrived at his apartment, he greeted me warmly as he opened the door. I walked in, and he closed the door behind me. He held my face gently in his hands and lifted my chin toward him. His right hand slid up the nape of my neck to the back of my hairline. I felt him grasp a handful of my hair as he pressed his body up against mine and kissed me passionately. His left hand began exploring my body. He traced the side of my exposed neck, my shoulders, and down the front of my body, gently tracing my breasts, then down to my waist, and over the curve of my hips. He pulled me closer to him as I responded with the same urgency I felt from him.

Without speaking, he lifted me up, carried me to the couch, and gently placed me on it. He slowly began to undress me, taking his time with each button on my shirt. He removed it slowly as he admired my body, leaving my bra on. He reached down to unfasten my jeans. He gently leaned me back and, with one swift gesture, took them off and left me in my underwear, lying nearly naked and full of lustful desire.

He removed his clothes to reveal a slender, sinewy body that was toned and strong. His soft blue eyes were accented by his fair hair and complexion. His skin was warm and soft, and his erection was hard, straining the beautiful pink color of his skin.

He moved toward me as I lay on the couch and gently brushed the tip of his cock against my lips. I parted my lips slightly in response, just to allow the tip to enter my mouth. It was warm, soft, and inviting. I opened my mouth, inviting him to go deeper, but he stopped. He warned me that he was close and that he may cum at any moment. I didn't care in that moment. As my tongue circled the tip of his cock, I felt him grow harder in my mouth. My whole body was vibrating with desire. I tilted my head to allow him to slide deeper into my mouth and turned slightly until he slid deep into my throat.

I could feel his whole body tensing just before he came into my mouth. I began teasing him with my tongue and throat, causing him to reach a full orgasm. To my utter surprise and delight, he tasted like pineapple; I wanted to drink every drop of him, filling my senses with the taste and memory of the pineapple he had placed in my mouth the week before.

He ran his hands over my body, removing my underwear, slowly admiring my curves. He began kissing my neck and ran his tongue down to my breasts, slowly and gently sucking on each nipple, making them erect with desire. As he moved down my stomach toward my clit, I could barely contain myself. I was wild with desire, and my hips began to move to meet his warm lips and tongue. He pressed my hips back into the couch to hold me still as he began gently flicking and sucking on me until I reached an explosive orgasm.

We lay in each other's arms for a few minutes, and I started to feel him getting hard against me again. He sat up on the couch, pulling me onto his lap, and guided himself into me, sliding easily into my eager, hot, wet body. I felt him grow harder as he began to move faster, positioning him perfectly to hit my g-spot with every thrust. I came hard and fast as he released, coming deep inside me. I held him tightly around the neck and kept my legs wrapped around his waist until the trembling of the intense orgasm we had just shared subsided.

We continued exploring each other for the rest of the day, finally falling into a light nap just before class. My hair was a mess, and I smelled like sex. I jumped into the shower, and, as I lathered up my body, the fragrance of the soap lit up my senses. This was his smell—clean and fresh. I felt myself getting excited again as I ran my hands over my soapy body. The shower curtain opened, and he stepped in behind me.

He lifted my arms over my head and turned me to face the wall of the shower. As he held my hands with one hand, I felt the fingers of his other hand slip inside me. I felt him begin to hard again, and he thrust himself inside me from behind. He came quick and hard this time, leaving me breathless, and a little sore. He gently turned me to face him as he lathered my body once again and gently rinsed me off.

As we made our way to class, I was very aware of how sore I was, and had to consciously move my body, and be mindful of my facial expressions so as not to give away our secret. After class, I went home and soaked in a warm bubble bath. That night I slipped into a deep, dreamless sleep.

After a few months of passionate sex, he asked me once again if I was open to a sensory game. At this point I trusted this man fully and completely, and it would never cross my mind to deny him whatever experience he wanted. This time, you will not only be blindfolded, but I also want to restrain you. He assured me that I was still in full control, and I could tell him to stop at any time.

He put me on my knees as he quickly and deftly tied my hands behind my back with the belt from his uniform. He then placed the black sash over my eyes. I was now without sight and unable to move my arms. I felt wildly vulnerable and excited. I felt him kiss me gently on the forehead as he told me to relax. He positioned himself behind me and began gently and sensually caressing my body. After months of being together, he had studied my body and my responses. He knew when and where to touch me to bring me over the edge in either minutes or hours, depending on his mood. I had become accustomed at that point to becoming quite submissive to him.

Between the lack of sight and the restraint of my movements, all of my other senses became heightened. He smelled as if he had just stepped out of the shower; that wonderful, warm fragrance of cloves filled my nostrils. I felt him run his hands down my spine, wandering over my ass. He began to slide his fingers into me from behind; I was wet and hot. I began breathing heavily and was not sure how much longer I could contain myself. Suddenly I felt his finger slip up into my ass. I gasped a little and felt my body tense up.

He asked if I was ok as he caressed me with his other hand, sliding his finger into me from the front, nearly bringing me to orgasm, and then stopping just before I came. I just nodded my head that I was ok. He asked if I had ever had anal sex, and I shook my head no. He said that he really wanted to explore it with me and asked if I was willing. I could barely hear his questions; my senses were exploding. I just wanted him to take me, and I didn't care how. He told me that I would have to relax my body and warned me that it may hurt, but he would be as gentle as possible.

As I felt him enter my body, I could feel intense pressure and some light pain. He instructed me to take a deep breath and relax my muscles. I did as I was told, and, with one last thrust, I felt him come deep inside me. He pulled out slowly, untied my hands, and removed my mask. Gently he turned me towards him and carefully cradled me in his arms. I rest my head on his chest and deeply breathed in his scent. He led me to the shower where he gently and respectfully washed me.

My mind was racing, and my body was sore. We got dressed and snuggled on the couch. After a long silence, he asked if that was an experience I would like to have again. I sat in silence for a moment, looking for the words to let him know how I was feeling. The experience was intense, slightly painful, and out of my comfort zone. I told him that I appreciated the patience and care he took with me, but it was not something that I wanted to do again. He thanked me for my honesty and trust and assured me we never would.

We continued our clandestine romance for a few months. The initial intensity of our physical relationship began to slow down. He was mostly focused on completing the work on his manual. I began studying energy healing and taking classes on the weekends. One weekend I attended a seminar in New Mexico at a Zen Center. It was peaceful and empowering. I had the opportunity to work with some of the monks who were practicing Tai Chi near the hot springs. Noticing that their structure was off, I offered to show them how to adjust their postures and stances. They were happy to have me show them, and I was honored to be of assistance.

Upon my return, I shared my experience with Teacher. He listened respectfully, then changed the subject, asking if we could turn our attention to the final draft and publication of his manual. He wanted to have copies ready for sale at the next seminar. A week before the seminar, the book was complete, and we had our first printing done. The class and the book were sold out. A few students asked about joining his weekly class. I directed them to Teacher and, upon his approval, gave them the information they would need to join us.

The classes were informal and by invitation only. Students came and went. One day in particular, a young man showed up to class. Full of wild, untamed energy, he possessed a youthful curiosity and enthusiasm that contrasted with the controlled energy of the others. Affectionately, we referred to him as "the twelve-year-old."

I first met him in class at the park. Teacher often gave new students to me to run through the basics during classes. That day we were practicing sensing hands. He was approximately six feet, one inch, and slender in build. His hair was dark, and he had brown eyes that had a playful gleam. When he lifted his wrists to touch mine, his energy felt like a bolt of electricity. At the signal to begin, I felt all his muscles tense at my touch instead of relaxing. Within seconds, I located his weak spot and gave him a small push; he fell to the ground with a thump.

The playful look in his eyes left rapidly and was replaced by disbelief; he looked up at me from the ground and, without thinking, called me a bitch. I just looked down at him, sitting before me. He was immediately horrified, and he apologized. I didn't take it personally; most men are not fond of being dumped on their ass by a small woman, especially with an audience of other men. With a warm smile, I assured him it was ok, and I offered him a hand.

The next class he arrived with a small sculpture of a fish. He told me it was a sign of good fortune, prosperity, and abundance, and a further apology for his rudeness the previous week. I accepted the gift graciously and let him know that it was just a part of the training. I assured him that I had been the one on the ground many times. It was simply a teachable moment, nothing more. He bowed to me ever so slightly and thanked me. I returned the gesture out of respect for his sincerity.

Teacher had been paying attention, as he always did, to our interactions and conversations. After class Teacher took me aside and promoted me, awarding me the title of instructor. I resisted, insisting I did not deserve that honor, and he was surprised I gave him a push back.

He said sarcastically and a little annoyed, "What do you need, a certificate of proof?"

"Yes," I said, perhaps a little more petulantly than I intended, and he just sighed. I knew he was only mildly irritated by his slight grin.

The next class, the twelve-year-old showed up with a small bouquet of flowers for me, and Teacher presented me with a beautifully inscribed and stamped certificate, naming me an itinerant monk and teacher. He recounted my adventures from my trip to New Mexico, where I taught monks correct postures and forms by the hot springs on a weekend retreat.

He laughed his deep, seductive laugh and said, "Only you would go on a retreat and come back sharing a story of teaching without even realizing it." He had shown such little interest when I shared my adventure with him. I had forgotten I told him that story.

Embarrassed by the attention, I shrugged and said, "I was watching them; I saw that their structure was out of line, and I didn't want them to get hurt." As I said the words, I realized he may be right. I was a teacher.

As he handed me the beautifully inscribed and detailed parchment, he leaned over and whispered in my ear, "Now it's official. You have your certificate. Don't argue with me."

I just laughed, and I'm sure I turned a brilliant shade of crimson as I humbly accepted the honor.

I began traveling quite a bit, embarking on a spiritual journey, and for the first time in a long time, I was beginning to feel that I had found a true calling. One trip in particular, I traveled to Peru for a ten-day journey where I met a holy man. He invited me to join him as a student. The training would be for twenty-one days, and it was by invitation only. I was excited to be one of twenty-five people from around the world invited on this journey.

I returned home, excited to share the news of what I considered to be a great honor and opportunity with Teacher. I thought he would be happy for me, but instead, he appeared agitated. I felt my heart sink at the thought of displeasing him.

He was becoming very possessive and, at times, a bit curt with me. When I asked him if I had done something wrong, he answered no, just that he was very unhappy that I was planning on leaving for twenty-one days. He told me that he was concerned that if I continued on the path of travel and trainings, I would be beyond his reach.

He said, "I will not be able to touch the hem of your robe." What he really meant was that he was losing control over me.

Suddenly the reality came crashing in on me. The confidence he once showed was veiled in intentional dominance. He had me convinced that by choosing to be submissive, I would always be in control. I would have the option to say no at any time.

Now that I began showing the slightest interest in something other than him and his goals, finally gaining some independence, he did not like it. He became envious, jealous, and unsupportive. I felt saddened that he was not at all interested in my personal growth but only interested in the control he had over me.

Our relationship was strained by my shifting attitude and his intolerance of it. I had been married to a man who wanted to control me, and I began to panic, thinking I was back in the same situation. I had no intention of slowing down or stunting my growth for anyone, and I was determined to follow my heart.

I was truly heartbroken and felt that a deep trust had been crushed. Realizing once again that I was involved in a situation where I was being dominated and controlled, my guard went up. I wondered if I would ever find anyone who would love and accept me. One thing I did know was that it was time to leave.

I told him that our relationship was over, and I wished him well. I thanked him for the training in class and the experiences we had. I was in control, and, as I walked away, he was speechless. I swore I would protect my heart by never allowing anyone to have that kind of control over me again.

Shower in Peru

My second trip to Peru became a two-day journey. My first flight was to Miami, where I was to catch a flight on Aero Peru to Lima and then a puddle jumper to Cuzco. After four delays and gate changes in Miami, our flight finally arrived in Lima late. We had to wait until the next morning for the next flight to Cuzco. As everyone gathered their luggage, mine was missing. The airline assured me that they would find it and deliver it to my hotel.

 I checked into my room and was feeling very grateful that I had chosen to book a single room. I was exhausted, and the last thing I wanted was to share my space with a stranger. I had my backpack, which thankfully contained my toiletries, a small bar of soap, and my hair brush. I had dressed in layers for the flight; I am not sure what possessed me to do this, but boy was I happy I did. At least I could mix things up and appear to have a change of clothes until they located my belongings.

As I lay my head down on the pillow, I felt grateful that I had the next three weeks to rest and recover from my last experience. I was determined to use this time to clear my mind and heal my heart. I had given myself willingly in hopes of finding reciprocated, unconditional love, only to be deceived once again. As I drifted off to sleep, the old tapes in my head began to play. I fought the feelings that I was somehow unlovable, damaged, and unworthy. Laying in the dark, I felt my eyes well up with tears as I silently cried myself to sleep.

The next morning our group met and all went to breakfast together. As we entered the dining room, we were greeted by the staff of servers and the chef. We enjoyed a light breakfast and then all settled in for a few days to allow our bodies to adjust to the change in altitude.

Our hotel was located next to the Urubamba River. The river was lined with eucalyptus trees. The sound of the water as it cascaded over the well-worn rocks was calming. I sat on the ground and leaned against a large boulder on the bank of the river, listening to the soothing sounds of the water and inhaling the clean, fresh scent of eucalyptus. The sounds of the river and the intoxicating scent of eucalyptus lulled me into a light trance-like state. I felt the sadness in my heart begin to melt away, and a feeling of hope and joy began to take its place.

Aromas from the kitchen filled the air, and the staff began preparing our lunch. I had just completed a six month training program that required me to eliminate any meat from my diet. I found that after eating "clean" for so long, my sense of smell and taste were heightened. Given my food restrictions,

I decided that it would be wise to speak to someone on the kitchen staff and request a cooked vegetarian meal if possible. When I entered the dining hall, the chef was there, preparing the luncheon for our group. I was grateful that he spoke English because I do not speak any Spanish.

This man was tall and slender with a gentle air about him. Most of the Peruvian men I had seen so far were rather short and a bit stout. He spoke with a heavy accent that made his words sound almost musical as they rolled off his tongue. I explained to him that I don't eat meat and would appreciate it if he could give me a warning when the buffet was served as to which dishes would be safe for me. He told me it would not be a problem and thanked me for letting him know.

At lunch the chef guided me to the dishes that were safe for me to eat. I had my first taste of quinoa with roasted vegetables. It was absolutely delicious. I thanked him once again and complimented him on his food. That night at dinner, he prepared a full vegetarian menu and told me later that he did that just for me. I was sincerely flattered that he took such special care to accommodate my needs.

That evening a bonfire near the river was planned for the group and the staff; he invited me to walk with him. We met and walked down together to find a seat near the fire. He shared with me that he had studied at a culinary school in California and wanted to return there someday to open his own restaurant. I enjoyed listening to him share his dreams with me. Sitting by the fire with the stars twinkling overhead and the sound of the water flowing over the rocks was very relaxing.

He was charming, intelligent, and a lovely companion for the evening. As the fire died, he walked me back to my room and asked if he could come inside. I told him, no. He respectfully thanked me for a nice evening and left without any resistance. I was grateful, and I made sure that my door was locked.

Early the next morning, the group left on our journey to the sacred sites and the beginning of our training. We spent the next few weeks traveling to various sacred sites. At the end of our travels, we returned to the same hotel the day before we were heading home. We arrived a little late and found the chef and his staff had the dining hall set up for a goodbye party for us. They had live music and a beautiful vegetarian spread.

We all celebrated our journey together, and the staff joined us on the dance floor for a final farewell. I was feeling grounded, relaxed, and joyful from our travels. Once again, I had stuffed the memories and secrets I held for so long, deep down in my soul. My heart was open to the promise and possibilities of new beginnings, and my thoughts were filled with hope.

After dinner a few of us went for a walk to sit by the river and soak up the last moments of this magical place. I excused myself, as I was feeling very dusty and tired. All I wanted was to take a shower and get some sleep before my journey home early the next morning.

The shower in my room was a large walk in shower. I turned on the water, and as the room filled with steam, I stepped in. I thought I heard a sound outside the bathroom door, but before I could check, the shower door opened, and the chef stepped in the shower with me. Standing there naked and smiling, he took me in his arms and kissed me. He told me that he could not stop thinking about me since we met, and he wanted to make love to me. My mind was reeling; it happened so quickly. Memories of the rape at Duck Pond flashed through my mind. I felt myself beginning to panic. I was in a single room that was not attached to any other rooms.

As I objected to him being there, I felt his hands slide over my wet, soapy skin, tracing the curves of my body and running his hand up the inside of my thigh. His touch was gentle and exciting. My body was betraying me. I had no desire to sleep with this man. All I could think was that I needed to take control of the situation. The words "don't resist, and you will not get hurt" were screaming in my mind.

Without thinking, I kissed him deeply to distract him, and then turned him around to face the wall. I lathered up his body, beginning at his neck and shoulders, and then ran my hands down his cut arms and muscular back, over his trim waist and perfect ass.

I reached around him, being sure to keep him facing the wall, and began soaping his chest and hard stomach as I slid my hands over his hips and down the front of his thighs. With one hand, I kept him facing away from me as I firmly took his cock in my other hand and began slowly stroking him until I felt him become so hard that he could not hold it any longer. He began meeting my strokes with intense thrusts gliding through my fingers. I felt his ass tighten against me; his body shook in my hands as he came. I felt his muscles relax with his release, and he turned to kiss me as the warm water cascaded over us. He was satisfied. He asked to stay, and I told him that I wanted to be alone; I had an early flight and asked him to please go. I locked the door behind him and collapsed on the bed as the rush of fear and adrenaline left my body.

The next morning he was there to bid us all goodbye and safe journeys home. He gave me a hug and kissed me on the cheek. My head was still reeling from the night before. I was grateful that things had not gotten out of my control and was happy to leave him and that strange encounter behind me.

I arrived in Miami and planned on visiting my mom for a few days. While I was there, the phone rang. My mother (who had the same name and nearly identical voice on the phone) answered and was greeted by a male voice with a heavy accent, deep and sensual, saying "Hello, it is me. I miss you, and I can't stop thinking of you."

I was on the other line as we picked up the phone at the same time.

There was a slight hesitation before I heard her respond, "I think you have the wrong person." She called for me to pick up the line and hung up when I said hello.

I heard the chef's voice asking me if I missed him. He told me that he wanted to move to California and be with me. I made it perfectly clear that I was not interested in a relationship or even seeing him again, for that matter. Warily, I asked him how he got that phone number, and he told me that it was on my registration card from the villa as an emergency contact. I insisted once again that I was not interested, and he finally said he understood and agreed not to contact me again.

The Younger Man

A few months after I returned from Peru, I started looking for a new place to study Tai Chi. A Chinese healing center had just opened in town, offering beginner classes; the instructor was a woman. I thought it would be nice to experience the forms being taught from a female perspective. After my last teacher and then my strange encounter with the chef in Peru, I was in dire need of some female energy.

Classes were open to the public. I went in one evening, a few minutes before class, to get a feel for the school. When class began, I respectfully took a place at the back of the room. We did some warm up exercises led by the instructor. She demonstrated a single posture, and we practiced the movement slowly and mindfully on her instruction. Toward the end of the class, she turned on a lovely sound track and took her place in front of the room, very much like classes with Sifu and Teacher; the class followed along.

She was teaching a form that I was familiar with, and I was able to relax into the energy of the class by following the instructor's pace. Her movements were fluid and graceful, and once again, I felt the calm energy of moving meditation flowing through me. It was the first time in a very long time that I was in an enclosed classroom. There were mirrors on every wall, allowing me to check and correct my posture from each angle.

I watched the instructor as closely as I was able from the back of the room. I caught her eye in the mirror once or twice, watching me as well as all the other students. At the end of the class, she approached me and asked why I had joined that class. I told her that I was looking for a class close to home. She shook her head and said, "But you are not a beginner. I can see by the way you move that you are more advanced than this class."

She asked if I would be willing to help with correcting the postures of new students, and in return, she would waive my class fees. I was flattered by her offer and humbly accepted it. After a few classes as her assistant, she offered me the opportunity to have a few private lessons to advance me to teacher. Feeling grateful to have found a new instructor, I told her that I would like that very much, and I began staying after class for one-on-one instruction. After a few weeks, she was comfortable giving me my own class times, and to compensate me, she would have me join her advanced class on Saturday mornings.

I was scheduled to teach introductory and beginner classes two nights a week. After a few weeks, I noticed some students showed up faithfully from week to week, and others just dropped in out of curiosity. I enjoyed working with new people as well as watching the more dedicated students learn and grow. One evening, as I was introducing myself to the class, the "twelve-year-old" from Teacher's class walked in. He looked as surprised to see me as I was to see him. I welcomed him to the class as I would any other new student and asked him to please find a place on the floor. After class he asked me why I had not been at the park. I told him that I had found this new instructor, and it was simply time for a change.

The next week just as we were about to begin, I heard the door open. I looked up to see him standing there with possibly the largest bouquet of wild flowers I have ever seen. He walked directly toward me and, without a word, presented them to me. I heard one of the male students in the back of the room make a comment that there was nothing any one of them could do to top that. He had a lightness in his voice that convinced me he was joking. A light chuckle went through the class, and I just shook my head a little and smiled. I thanked him, quickly put the flowers down on a nearby table, and once again asked him to take a spot on the floor.

I proceeded to teach the class, being mindful to pay close attention to the other students and purposely making him wait if he had any questions. After class he told me that he would like to spend some time with me, and he asked me out for coffee. I thanked him for the flowers and politely refused his invitation. I really had no interest in even a coffee date with this young man.

For the next few weeks, he came to class, and after each class, he would ask me to go for coffee. This young man was persistent. I finally agreed to have coffee with him after his fifth request. He sat across from me and never broke eye contact as we talked. He was thirteen years younger, tall, dark, and handsome with a sparkling smile and twinkling eyes. What I could not understand was why in the world he would be interested in spending time with me.

With great respect and sincerity, he said to me, "All your lines go up."

I just looked at him and raised my brows a little, saying, "Excuse me?"

He quickly continued that he felt when a woman reaches a certain age, you can see in her face what she is like. I just shook my head a little; this was either the best or worst line I had ever been given. I gave him the opportunity to clarify himself before I decided.

He gave me an impish smile and continued to explain that he felt girls his age only cared about their hair and their clothes. They have no idea who they are yet or what they want. Their faces are smooth and don't yet tell a story; they are blank.

"When I look at you, I can see a map that shows me you are a happy person, who is comfortable with who she is, because all your lines go up."

By now, I was, in fact smiling. He just smiled back. I laughed a little at this artful explanation and said, "Good save. That was the best line I have ever heard!"

I agreed to go on a date with him because of his sheer persistence and a little curiosity. On our first date, he told me that he wanted to have "the sex talk." This should have been my first red flag that I was entering a world I may not understand.

We were, after all, more than a decade apart in age. I told him he would have to take the lead as I had no idea what he was talking about.

He said, "Is there anything I should know about you before we have sex?"

Surprised by his question, I asked him if he was under the impression that we were going to have sex. He said yes, and I just laughed, letting him know that he was being very presumptuous.

He asked again, and I responded, "No, and I asked if there was anything I should know?"

He replied, "Yes, I have a really big dick."

Certain that he was attempting to shock me, I laughed and asked him if that was a warning or I was supposed to be impressed.

He smiled and said, "It was a warning."

Without hesitation, I responded, "Well, if we ever get there, I hope you know what to do with it, because it has been my experience that bigger is not always better. First, let's see how you date before we continue that conversation."

After a few more dates and deeper conversations, he proved to be mature beyond his years in some areas. He graduated from The Berkley School of Music, majoring in piano, both classical and jazz. I confessed that classical piano was a favorite of mine. He told me that one of his old professors was working at a local piano bar and invited me there for drinks. I was truly intrigued. This was a much different side to him than the wild energy I first met in the parking lot at Teacher's class.

When we arrived, he was greeted warmly by his former professor and mentor. We took a seat at the piano bar and ordered a drink. In between sets they chatted happily together. Just before he was about to begin his last set of the evening, he invited his former student to play and introduced him to the late night crowd. Everyone in the bar welcomed him with a round of polite applause to encourage him to play.

I was very interested in hearing him play. He smiled at me and said, "How does a piece by Rachmaninoff appeal to you?"

His mentor took his seat beside me and said, "Watch this."

I watched as he transformed before my eyes from a wild child to a master pianist. With one deep breath, he positioned himself at the piano, placed his fingers on the keys, closed his eyes, and began to flawlessly, from memory, play one of the most romantic pieces I had ever heard. The entire bar became quieter with each note he played until the room was only filled with the sweet melody he was playing.

I was mesmerized by the music and the knowledge that this performance was for me. It made me feel quite special. He gently played the last note, opened his eyes, looked directly at me, and smiled. He was met with a roar of enthusiastic applause from every person in the bar. He politely thanked the audience and returned to his seat next to me. I felt as if I was seeing him for the first time. Clearly this young man had many layers. That night he most definitely had my attention.

We began dating, and unfortunately, his assumption that having a large dick would be enough to satisfy someone in bed was a mistake, though his youth and enthusiasm helped make up for his lack of experience. He was willing and eager to learn, and I found myself in the unique position of being the teacher in the bedroom, not a role that I had much experience or interest in. Soon I found myself craving the company and companionship of a more mature and experienced lover. Someone with self-discipline and skills that only age and experience could provide.

I began to pull away from him. I noticed drastic changes in his normally wild yet playful energy to a darker side. He was showing signs of insecurity and possessiveness, making passive aggressive comments that he may meet someone younger at any time and leave me. Honestly I was beginning to feel that it would be a relief if he did. Not getting the reaction he was expecting, he would then rapidly change the conversation. He would then profess his love for me and desire to marry me. I told him honestly that I had no intention of ever getting married again.

This drastic, contrasting, and erratic behavior seemed to be happening more and more. First he was on top of the world, filled with joy and wonder, and then without warning, he was pensively pondering what the point of everything was. These emotional swings began to make me feel incredibly uncomfortable and on edge.

One day, I found him in a particularly dark mood, and I asked him what was truly wrong. He shared with me that when he was young, he was diagnosed as being bipolar. This would definitely account for his drastic mood swings. He told me that he tried to take medication once when he was younger, but he didn't like the way it made him feel, so he never took it again. He confessed that he had been battling the mood swings for months, hoping I would not notice, but he felt like he was losing control. I suggested he see a professional to help him out, and he refused. I was at a loss as to how to help him if he refused to help himself.

After a few weeks, the darker moods seemed to be more frequent. The good moods, laced with what once seemed like joy, were beginning to resemble a kind of wild frenzy. It became increasingly difficult to be with him until one day he simply became too dark for me to handle.

He came to my house, looked me in the eye, and told me he was going to kill himself. I'm not sure what he was looking for as a response to this declaration, but this was too dark for me to handle. I went into an immediate mode of self-preservation. I called his brother, told him what he had just told me, and asked him to please come to my house and get him. His family was aware of his illness and this behavior, and it was time for them to step up and get him the help he needed.

When his brother arrived, with him as my witness, I said I was not willing to be with someone who would choose doing themselves harm over getting the help they need. There was nothing I could do to help him. I was done, and I did not want to have any further contact with him.

When he started to object, his brother gently took him by the arm and said, "It's over. It's time for you to come with me now."

As the door closed behind them, I felt an overwhelming sense of relief. For the first time in months, I felt my body relax. I had not realized until that moment how much his darkness was affecting me. My guard went up once again in an attempt to keep myself safe and have some peace of mind.

The Tall, Dark, and Handsome Stranger

After my experience with the younger man, I was feeling like it would be best if I spent some time on my own. When I wanted to go out, I was perfectly capable of being my own date. There was a lovely local steakhouse where I could sit at the bar, have a glass of wine, and listen to live music. I had made friends with the bartender, and he offered to assist me if I had any unwanted attention or felt unsafe leaving at the end of the evening. I appreciated this extra service and having a place to go where I felt safe. I positioned myself at the end of the bar with a wall to one side of me and placed my purse on the stool next to me to create an invisible barrier.

Seats at the bar began filling up as the band began playing. I heard a deep male voice behind me asking, "Is this seat taken?" I was prepared to say yes, just to keep a safe distance from any unwanted conversation. I turned around and found myself looking into a pair of dazzling hazel eyes and a handsome face with full lips and thick, dark hair. He looked to be around my age, over six feet tall, and nicely dressed.

I didn't answer right away, so he asked again, "Is this seat taken?"

I hesitantly lifted my purse up, offered him the spot next to me, and turned my attention back to my wine and the music while waiting for my dinner to arrive.

He asked me why I was there alone and I answered, "I came for the music and dinner."

I did my best to simply ignore him, but he was determined to start a conversation with me. I told him that I had just ended a relationship and was perfectly content with my own company. He ordered himself dinner, and we sat quietly next to each other, listening to the music. He offered to buy me a drink after dinner, and I accepted. We had some light conversation, and when the music ended, he offered to walk me to my car. I said, "No, thank you," and he asked if I would be there again the following weekend. I told him I was not sure, but it was possible. As we said goodnight, he asked for my phone number, and I told him no, so he offered his instead. I took it and told him not to expect me to call, but perhaps we would run into each other again sometime.

A few weeks passed, and there was a blues band playing at the steakhouse that I wanted to hear. I got dressed and left a little early to be sure my favorite stool at the bar would be available, as well as the seat next to mine. When I arrived, I was greeted by my favorite bartender, who informed me that the dark haired stranger had been coming in, asking if he had seen me. He told me that he had a few conversations with him, and he seemed like an ok guy. I thanked him for letting me know.

I ordered my dinner and a glass of wine and listened to the sounds of the band warming up, feeling peaceful and content. Then I heard the familiar, deep voice ask if the seat next to me was taken. When I looked up, he smiled at me and told me that he had been back a few times, hoping to see me. He said he was disappointed that I didn't call.

"Well," I responded, "I told you not to expect a call," with a slight grin.

He laughed and said, "Yes, you did."

He took the seat next to me, ordered his own dinner, and we sat and listened to the music.

With the slow, melancholy sounds of the blues combined with the wine, I felt myself relaxing. He asked me if I would like to dance, and I accepted. He took me in his arms, and I rested my head comfortably on his chest as we swayed gently with the music. His strong arms held me close to him and felt warm and inviting. It had been a long time since my last relationship.

When the music ended and the bartender called last call, it was time to leave, and he offered to walk me to my car. I accepted, and this time when he asked if I would call, I said yes. He took me once again into his arms and kissed me goodnight. His kiss was warm and gentle, stirring feelings of desire I had not felt for some time.

I called him a few days later, and we made arrangements to meet at a bar the next weekend. When the day arrived, I found myself taking extra care to get ready for the evening. I was interested in this man, but I was feeling vulnerable. I was not interested in a relationship, yet I was wildly attracted to him.

Once again, we shared some drinks and had an easy, light conversation. He really didn't talk too much about himself or his past, and I did not offer him much information about mine. I enjoyed his company. I could feel my walls coming down slowly. At the end of the evening, he walked me to my car and told me he would call me soon. His good night kiss was deeper and more passionate. My body was filled with intense, sudden desire. That night, when I lay down to sleep, my mind drifted off thinking about what it would be like to feel him inside me.

He began to make it a habit to call during his lunch break just to say hello and that he was thinking of me. I liked the attention he was giving me, and I looked forward to hearing how the day was going. After a few weeks, he invited me out for something to eat and a ride to the country side to go leaf peeping. We took separate cars and met at a Chinese restaurant he chose. We shared a scorpion bowl and a light appetizer sitting side by side in a booth in the back. He was becoming very affectionate, so I suggested we take our adventure on the road and enjoy the leaves that were at full peak.

We drove around lazily, looking at the leaves. I simply adore the changing of the leaves. The brilliant colors of autumn driving down a country road are truly something to admire. We came to a curve in the road with a small parking area marked with a sign that read "Scenic View." I asked him to pull over and got out of the car to take a moment to enjoy the fresh air and the breathtaking view.

The sun was warm on my skin, but there was crispness in the air. I wore a comfortable, flowing dress. As a small breeze passed by, I felt the hem of my dress lift gently and then settle back in place. Out of the corner of my eye, I noticed the quick, small smile on his face as he watched my dress rise just a little.

I was leaning over the hood of the car, resting my chin in my hands, soaking in the magnificent view when I felt his hands on my back. They were warm and strong. As he moved closer to me, he pressed against me from behind. I felt him getting hard as his hands slid down the sides of my body, resting on my hips. He leaned down and began kissing the nape of my neck.

I arched my back slightly and felt my body tingling as my breath began to quicken. I felt him lift up my dress from behind. He had me leaning over the hood of the car as I felt him slide into me slowly and firmly. As my body responded, he began to quicken his thrusts. He was in the perfect position inside me; I began losing myself in the moment. The air was a little cool, and the sun was warm on my face. As I began to feel myself about to climax, I felt his body tense as he thrust hard and deep inside me. I felt him come inside me as he held me closer. He did not let go for a few moments. We both stayed still in that position while we caught our breath.

As our bodies settled down, I knew I would never forget the smell of the autumn air, the sun on my face, and this man filling every inch of me. We continued our leaf peeping adventure in silence and then returned to the parking lot of the restaurant. He kissed me sweetly, and we said our goodbyes.

Over the next few weeks, we spent more time together, yet we still enjoyed time away from each other. I had a strong desire to be in control of my personal time and explore my own sensuality. He was not intimidated by it. In fact, he admitted that he enjoyed it. I felt a sense of personal freedom that was strangely empowering. He had awakened a free spirited playfulness in me.

The more time we spent together, our relationship became more intimate, yet it never lasted longer than the length of a date or intense sex. I was beginning to want more. Every time I began talking about spending more time together, he seemed to sidestep the conversation, or he used the excuse of having conflicts with work.

Then, the perfect opportunity arose for me to surprise him and enjoy some time together. He told me he was going out of town to visit his family in Canada. I asked to see his flight itinerary, and after I saw the dates and times, I offered to give him a ride to and from the airport. He thanked me but said that he would make ride arrangements. He told me how much he would miss me and would let me know as soon as he returned.

When I looked at the itinerary, I quickly noted the airline, flight, and his return seat number. I thought to myself, mischievously, how much fun and exciting it would be to fly there for a surprise. After he left, I called my travel agent and had her book me a flight a little later the same day, on the same flight as his return, as well as the seat next to him.

The hotel I booked had a beautiful indoor pool, a bar, and a Japanese steak house all within the hotel. I was only going to be there for a few days, so I was able to pack everything in a small carry-on. When I arrived at the hotel and got settled into my room, I called him to let him know that I was there. It was my intention for this to be a grand romantic gesture.

When he answered the phone, I told him that I was at a hotel near the airport. There was a moment of silence. He sounded surprised but not pleased. My hopes of a romantic weekend were dashed by the hesitation in his voice. I did after all surprise him with this visit. I decided to leave the option for him to join me, open. Regardless, I was there for an adventure, happy to explore and enjoy myself.

I gave him the name of the hotel where I was staying, and I invited him to meet me for a drink or dinner. He told me that he had family obligations and wasn't sure when he would be able to see me. I assured him it was quite fine. I understood that it was a surprise, and I had already made arrangements to entertain myself. I made a reservation at the steakhouse for dinner that evening, leaving me time for a quick dip in the pool and some relaxation in the hot tub before going to the bar for a cocktail. He knew my plans for the evening and where to find me if he could get away and we left it at that.

I got into my bathing suit and went down to the pool. I could smell the chlorine as I walked down the hallway, and I was greeted with warm, balmy air as I opened the door to the pool area. The pool water was clear and inviting, with a beautiful six person hot tub next to it. I was the only one in the water, so I swam a few leisurely laps and then simply floated for a little while. I moved into the hot tub, and as I immersed myself slowly and completely, I felt the warm water caressing my body. The multiple streams of jets massaged my neck, shoulders, and back. It felt glorious, and all the muscles in my body began to relax. I closed my eyes. My mind began to drift and become calm.

I returned to my room and took a hot, steamy shower. I lathered up my long, dark hair and then took the extra time to leave in a deep conditioner. I never seemed to take the time to do this at home for some reason. This weekend I decided to pamper myself. I hadn't taken a vacation in years and had never been to Canada. I was on an adventure and excited to see where it would take me.

I took my time drying my hair, applying my makeup, and getting dressed. When I was packing, I chose outfits that made me feel beautiful, desirable, and powerful. I began getting dressed, slowly and mindfully. First, I chose my lacey, black lingerie. The bra gently cradled my breasts and lifted them slightly. I slid on a pair of off-black crotch-less stockings that seductively caressed the curves of my hips. I carefully slid into the perfect little black dress I had chosen and zipped myself up.

When I looked in the mirror, I was pleased to see how the neckline came low enough to show my cleavage, but it left even more to the imagination. It was a simple A-line dress that fit my body perfectly. You know the one; you put it on, and it always makes you feel amazing. I stepped into a pair of five-inch stiletto pumps with a small open toe. I was ready to enjoy a cocktail and my evening.

While traveling alone, I learned to take certain precautions. When I checked in, I asked for two keys, saying that my husband would be joining me a little later. When and if I had room service, I always ordered enough food for two. With the shower running and the door open just a little, I would call out that our food was here. I wanted to give the server the impression that someone was in the room with me. I did not want a repeat of what happened in Peru.

I took a seat facing the door and introduced myself to the bartender. I placed my purse on the chair next to me to discourage anyone from sitting there, in hopes of my friend showing up. As I was placing my drink order, I noticed him standing in the doorway, just gazing at me. He walked over to me, took the seat next to me, and gave me a quick kiss on the cheek. He said he was really happy to see me but wasn't sure how much time he would have, explaining he was there for some family events. I told him I understood. When I booked this trip, I knew there would be a chance he would be busy.

He paid for my drink and offered to walk me back to my room. I reminded him that I had a dinner reservation at the steak house that I was very much looking forward to. He didn't seem pleased that I was going to dine without him, but he had his plans, and I made mine. He walked me to the door of the steak house, and we said good night.

I enjoyed a filet mignon and vegetables that were perfectly grilled. The people at the table were all very relaxed, and it was a fun show. I had a wonderful evening enjoying the company of these fun loving strangers.

After a lovely dinner and a few glasses of wine, I went up to my room and sat down to relax before going to sleep; suddenly there was a knock on the door. I looked through the peep hole, and there he was. I opened the door, and he walked in. He closed the door behind him as he lifted me up in the air. He kissed me deeply and intensely as he carried me over to the bed. As he slid his hand up my dress, he realized I was wearing crotchless stockings, and he had a look of surprise. He smiled and ran his hands along the soft stockings to my bare skin, teasing me with his fingers while he held me tight with the other arm, kissing me this time a little harder and more urgently.

As he pressed me against the bed with the weight of his body, he took off his pants. He was hard and ready. He reached down with both hands and held my hips as he thrust himself inside of me. I was so wet from him playing inside me with his fingers that he was able to be fully inside me in one thrust. I wrapped my arms around his shoulders and began to feel all the muscles in his back begin to tighten. He pulled out of me a little and then thrust himself deep inside me again, holding himself there. I began to wiggle my hips a little, and he told me to stop. He was too close; he needed a moment to calm himself.

He started a slow rhythm of sliding in and out of me, and I felt him getting hard inside of me again. Each time he entered into me, he went a little deeper. I met his slow thrusts with my hips and then positioned myself so he could get even deeper. His body began to tense again, and I knew he was ready to release. I allowed myself to completely relax into his rhythm when suddenly and intensely, we both came hard and strong.

As we collapsed into each other's arms, I looked down at him as he lay resting in my arms. He looked peaceful. My body was a little sore, but I was happy. After a short time, he got up, and I asked if he could stay. He said no; he had to be home for something with his parents in the morning, but he would call me later and take me for a drive to see some sights the next day.

After he kissed me good night and left, I got washed up and ready for bed. I was very tired from all the travel, dinner, and intense sex we just had. I fell into a deep, dreamless sleep. The next morning I had an early wake-up call. I ordered breakfast for two with mimosas and browsed leisurely through the travel pamphlets, waiting for his call. There was a tour going to Niagara Falls that looked like a lot of fun. I checked the times the tour bus was leaving.

The phone rang about 9:00 a.m., and he told me that he was going to be tied up for a few hours, and then he would be free to come and pick me up.

I said, "It depends on what a few hours means. I was thinking of taking a tour to go see Niagara Falls that leaves the hotel at 1:00 p.m."

He asked me to wait, and he would take me. I let him know that it was also my time off, and I was not ok spending the short precious time I had waiting for him. He promised to pick me up by noon.

We left the hotel at noon and drove through some breathtaking countryside roads. It was a beautiful day. The sky was blue with just a few puffy clouds gently floating in the air. The sun warmed my skin through the window. I enjoyed listening to him give me a tour of the area. He showed me where he grew up, pointing out vineyards that produced local ice wines, and told me about his grandfather's vineyard.

We arrived at Niagara Falls in the early afternoon. The magnificence, power, and beauty of the falls were awesome, stunning, and surreal. The thunderous sound of the falls and the view of the water crashing into a great pool below were mesmerizing. In the middle of the pool below was a boat, filled with tourists in yellow raincoats to protect them from the spray of water crashing down around them.

We decided to take the "Journey Behind the Falls" walking tour that brought us behind the cascading waterfall. Being so close to the rushing water was intense and invigorating. You could feel the sheer force of the water as it raced past you, crashing below. As the sun's rays shone through the water, I noticed small, fleeting rainbows that seemed to magically appear, only to be dashed away a moment later. The cool mist combined with the roaring sound of the falls filled my senses, and it was intoxicating.

I was having a wonderful time, and I wanted to capture the moment. I asked a fellow tourist if they would take our picture, and he objected. He said he didn't want his picture taken and offered to take one of me instead. I was a little taken aback by this reaction. He seemed a little annoyed by what I thought was an innocent request.

We decided that since it was a long drive back and we were both tired, it was time to head back to the hotel. When we got back, he told me he could not stay. He asked if he could come back that evening to see me. I told him to call me first as I may not be in the room.

He asked where I might be, and I said, "It depends on what time you plan on returning. I may be having a drink at the bar." He said he would find me. He watched as I left the car, waited as I entered the hotel, and then drove away.

I was feeling as though something had shifted between us. This trip, though planned as a grand romantic gesture on my part, was instead serving as a stark realization that any feelings I may have begun to feel for this man were not returned. I was beginning to wonder why he was never available at home either.

He called later that night, said that he could not get away, and asked what flight I was on. This was going to be the last of my planned surprises. He said, "I'm on the same flight, but someone in his family was giving him a ride to the airport, so he would see me at the gate."

I called the front desk and made arrangements for a ride to the airport the next morning. As I got ready for bed, my mind was racing. The entire weekend he was a bit distant and cool. The sex had been fast, hard, and a bit raw. I was interested to see how he would react to me having the seat beside him on the flight home.

The next morning, I packed and put on my intended travel outfit. I had chosen a long, loose-fitting dress that accentuated my waist as it gently rested on my curves. I made a point to arrive early and check in so I could see his reaction to seeing me when he arrived. We made eye contact as he walked into the check in area, and he walked right by me, straight to the counter.

After he checked in for his seat assignment, he took the seat next to me. He said good morning and asked where I was sitting.

I showed him my ticket, and he said, "That is next to me!"

"I know," I said, smiling sweetly at him. I felt like I was getting wild, mixed messages at this point.

He seemed edgy and a little uncomfortable.

It was a full flight that morning. We boarded the plane and found our seats. We were on the side of the plane that had two seats. I took the seat by the window and asked him to pull a blanket down for me from the overhead. As the plane took off, I laid the blanket over my lap and his. This was my last planned effort to surprise him.

He said he wasn't cold, and I whispered in his ear, "It is for privacy, not comfort."

He looked at me a little confused, then felt my finger gently trace the inside of his thigh. As I got closer to his crotch, I could feel the heat beginning to rise in him. He was getting hard as he responded quickly to my touch.

He whispered in my ear, "What are you doing?"

I just smiled, unzipped his jeans, and reached for him. He felt warm and smooth in my hand as I slowly and gracefully began stroking and bringing him into a full, hard erection. He put his hand on mine as if to stop me, and I just shook my head no. He came with a shuddering, silent release. I shifted the rest of the blanket onto his lap so he could gather, compose, and put himself back together discreetly.

He held my hand, and we sat quietly. I felt the same distant coolness that I had been feeling the day before. I had the feeling that I was a bit inconvenient for him. I shared with him how I was feeling. He did not respond. Suddenly all of the pieces seemed to fall together for me. I looked over at him and, without warning, asked him the question that had been gnawing at me all night.

"Are you married?"

He looked me in the eye, and without a second of hesitation or remorse, he just said, "Yes."

We sat in silence for a few moments, and it was deafening to me. He did not deserve me, and I certainly deserved to be treated much better than this. I was so concerned with not losing myself that I ignored all the signs. I was not interested in any relationship that made me a second thought, far less a cheater. I was beyond furious with him and myself.

He then told me that he wasn't sure if there would be someone meeting him at the gate. Quietly and coldly, I let him know that when we walked off the plane, it would be as if we had never met. He tried to tell me that he didn't want that, and I told him, "It really doesn't matter at this point what you want." I was done. As we disembarked from the plane, I wheeled my bag easily behind me and headed straight for the exit. I never looked back. I blocked his number and never spoke to him again.

The Match Date

I was visiting a friend who was recently divorced and ready to get out into the dating world. She had just joined Match and wanted me to join as well. I insisted that I was fine; it was not something that I wanted to get involved with. After the last experience I had, I thought it best to walk away from relationships. I was comfortable being single, but she was on the hunt and wanted support and company.

After a few glasses of wine and her relentless insistence, I agreed to allow her to set up a profile for me. I chose an extremely unflattering picture of myself and wrote a profile that read, according to her, more like a dare to contact me than an invitation. She attempted to rewrite my introduction, and I stopped her. I explained to her that I was in a space that would be challenging for anyone to engage with, and what I had written was honest.

She had no idea what my history with dating and relationships was aside from my marriage, and that was the only experience we had shared. There was no reason to tell her, as it was, after all, safer to keep it a secret. This I had learned from experience.

After a few disastrous dates, I decided that I was done. I had been lied to, stood up, and left to pick up the bill. On top of that, although my profile picture was not flattering, at least it was current. There was one profile that I thought was interesting. If the picture was true, the man had a nice smile and was attractive. I sent him a short note. He responded politely, but with what I considered little interest. I decided that it was time for me to leave the site; I had experienced enough deceit and disappointment. I sent him a short note to let him know that I would be leaving the match, and I wished him the best of luck.

I got an immediate response from him, asking why I was leaving and saying that we didn't even have a chance to chat. I was amused by this and let him know that he did not seem interested. After a few more messages, I agreed to talk with him on the phone.

He had a pleasant voice and seemed like a positive, genuinely fun person. After a week of conversation, he told me that he would be at a Chinese restaurant in the area that night. He asked me if I was interested in having a drink. I agreed to meet him at the bar.

I walked in and spotted him at a table in the corner. This was a good start; he actually looked like his picture. He was sitting with another man and two children. He didn't see me come in, so I went to the bar and ordered myself a drink. I took a seat at the table next to his and didn't say anything, watching out of the corner of my eye as he was talking with his friend. He looked over at me and smiled; I returned his smile and watched his face as he recognized me. He invited me to come and sit at his table and introduced me to his two children and his best friend. Everyone was very welcoming, but when his friend asked how we knew each other, his response was, "Work." I just looked at him in disbelief. I neither confirmed nor denied the statement and dodged any further questions, as I was not going to lie for this person.

I finished my drink, thanked them all for inviting me to join them, and started to walk out of the restaurant. He followed me, calling for me to please wait."

What the hell was that?" I asked. He said that he panicked and wasn't sure how to introduce me to his children. He made the comment that I looked a lot prettier in person than the profile picture. Apparently, his intention was to meet me so my feelings wouldn't be hurt, then let me know he was not interested. He was using his friend and children as a safety buffer. My first thought was that he was shallow and a liar—not a good first impression.

I let him ramble on for a few moments before he asked me to please forgive him and give him a second chance. He seemed sincere in his apology. Hesitantly I agreed to give him a second chance and met him the following night for an early dinner.

I walked into the restaurant and saw him sitting at a table, waiting for me. We ordered drinks, and he started the conversation with the question, "Are you magic?"

I just shook my head a little and responded, "What?"

He said, "It was a simple question: are you magic?"

I shrugged my shoulders slightly and said, "Yes, I am."

What an odd question to begin a date with. I had my guard up, as these were now two really strange encounters with this person. I had a bad track record with Match and, quite frankly, all men up until then.

The rest of the evening was very nice; we chatted and enjoyed our dinner. He walked me to my car and gave me a sweet, respectful goodnight kiss. He asked if he could see me again, and I agreed. He was pleasant, had a fun personality, and I was willing to see if it would go any further.

On our next date, I met him at a sports bar that he and some friends frequented. I am not a huge sports fan, and this was only the third time I met him in person. Given my previous match date disasters, I wanted to have a way out if need be.

The room was very loud and crowded. When I walked in, I spotted him at the bar, chatting with another man. I made my way over to him, and he offered me his seat. The three of us chatted and had a few drinks and some appetizers. They made me feel very welcome and comfortable. His friend seemed nice and polite. When the evening ended, he walked me to my car where we sat and continued our conversation. He asked if he could see me the following weekend. I told him to call me, and we would make arrangements.

Each day he texted and called me just to say hello and chat about our days. I was not used to this level of attentiveness, it was rather flattering. I enjoyed his conversation and hearing about his day, and he listened equally and intently to my recounts as well. I started to feel very comfortable with our daily routine and was looking forward to our next date. I agreed to let him pick me up at my house.

I was ready and waiting when the bell rang, but I did not invite him in. We went directly to dinner and had a very nice evening. Conversation turned to both of our previous marriages, and we somewhat bonded over the bad experiences we had with our ex's. I had, at this point, been single for a number of years. His recounting of his ex and the level of animosity he held for her led me to believe that his divorce was fairly recent.

We had quite a few cocktails and when he drove me home, what began as an innocent kiss goodnight, became much more heated. After some very intense foreplay, we glanced at the clock and realized hours had gone by. We both had early mornings, so we decided to say our goodbyes and revisit this at a later date. He walked me to the door and gave me one last deep kiss, leaving me feeling very hot and bothered. I was certain that I had done the same to him and wondered, as I fell asleep that night, where this would go.

Another week passed, and our phone conversations became more intimate. I was starting to feel extremely comfortable with this man and was looking forward to our next date. He took me out for drinks and dancing and asked if I would like to come to his apartment, which was right down the street. He must have felt me tense up, or maybe it was some unconscious look I gave him. He just laughed and joked that he lived next to the police station, so I would be safe. There was something about the way he said it that made me laugh also. I had quite a bit to drink, and, although I had my own car, it seemed much safer not to drive, so I agreed.

When we got to his apartment, he offered me a night cap. We sat on the couch. We began kissing and picked up where we had left off in the front seat of his car a week ago. That, combined with an overabundance of alcohol, caused my walls to come tumbling down. The next thing I remember was waking up on the couch, our naked bodies tangled in an awkward embrace. My first thought was, how much did I have to drink? My head was pounding from a massive hangover. I barely remembered what happened after we left the bar. I was getting dressed and heard his phone ring in the other room. He answered it as he walked into the room where I was. I heard him tell the person on the other end that he would not be able to meet them that evening. He said, "I think I have found the one." He looked at me and smiled.

After he hung up, he told me that he was ready to delete his profile and asked if we could see each other exclusively. I had already deleted my profile before we had our first date. I was tired of the insanity of internet dating and had come to a place where I was ready to admit defeat with relationships. I was confused as to why he would say he had found "the one," but I was willing to give it one more try. I enjoyed his company and was clearly attracted to him, so I agreed.

A month into our relationship, he began spending the night at my house. One evening he made plans for us to meet with the friend that I had met at the sports bar on our second date. He was as charming and pleasant as the first time we met. We were all very relaxed and having a good time. I noticed that my new boyfriend was very protective of me, which made me feel safe. This was a nice feeling, and I felt myself beginning to relax.

That night when he was driving me home, he was chatting suddenly about an ex-girlfriend of his. He shared with me that she had a threesome with him and the friend we had just left at the bar. He went on to say how hot it was and asked if I would be open to doing that.

My heart skipped a beat as feelings of shame washed over me like a tidal wave. I felt wildly disrespected and began to have flash backs of being passed from one man to another when I was younger. Strong feelings of fear, anger, and betrayal rose up in me.

I told him without hesitation, "That is a strong no!" If that was a deal-breaker for him, then we could just say good-bye right then and there.

He said he was sorry and that he would never bring it up again. That night I had him drop me off, and I sent him on his way. I needed time to recover from that conversation. I knew that he did not know my history, but I was having an intense reaction that I needed to sit with. The next day he called and apologized once more, promising that the subject would never come up again.

I warily agreed to continue seeing him; he was true to his word and was very respectful in regard to certain boundaries that I would not allow to be crossed. Once again, I felt my guard go up, but I slowly shared some of the experiences I had in the past. He became even more attentive and appeared protective of me.

After some time, I started to feel safe with him again. He reintroduced me to his children, but this time as his girlfriend. They began to join us on outings when he had time with them, and we all became comfortable with each other's company. I was introduced to and welcomed into his circle of friends and their girlfriends. For the first time, I felt at ease and accepted by a group of people.

We fell into a pleasant routine of spending time with his kids every other weekend. Just before Christmas, he told me that his ex-wife was threatening to take his children from him. He lived in a one bedroom apartment, and, according to the courts, his children needed to have rooms of their own in order for them to stay with him. He could not afford rent for a larger apartment in the area and told me he would have to consider moving.

My house had three bedrooms—more than enough room for him to share my room and for each of his children to have their own rooms when they stayed with him every other weekend. We had been spending quite a bit of time together; the only time he seemed to be at his apartment was when he had his children. I felt as if, for the first time in my life, I had what appeared to be a normal relationship. I offered to let him move in with me.

As we were packing up his apartment, he told me that there was something he needed to share with me. A little nervous about what may come next, I warily asked him "What?"

He told me that he had a rifle and enjoyed shooting. He wanted to be sure I was ok with having a firearm in the house. I was not sure why this topic had never come up in all the months we had been dating. I was not certain how I felt about it.

Aside from shooting a rifle at camp when I was young, I had no knowledge or experience with it. I would have to know more about it before I formed an opinion. He offered to arrange a private lesson for me with a certified instructor, and I agreed. The instructor was a friend of his who was also a range safety officer. I appreciated the time he took to explain everything from safe handling to range etiquette. He patiently answered my questions and concerns and guided me through my first shooting experience in decades. I left feeling much less apprehensive, but I told them that I would need more instruction to feel truly comfortable.

We visited sporting clubs with firing ranges close to where I lived, and after seeing quite a few, I agreed to one that I felt comfortable at. We joined the club that offered a class that was taught by instructors and designed specifically to teach women.

In the first part of the day, I learned about the safe handling and storage of various firearms, as well as the laws of the state. The class was designed for beginners, and I appreciated the in-depth information as well as the presentation. In the second half of the day, we had the opportunity to try out various caliber rifles, pistols, and shotguns. That afternoon I was introduced to target shooting, long-range rifle shooting, trap, and skeet. The instructors worked with each one of us individually at each station. This was a whole new world for me. I felt safe and, in fact, had a lot of fun. I decided I was interested in learning even more. At the end of the day, each person in the class was awarded a certificate of training that qualified us to apply for our class A License to Carry.

After class I thanked the instructor for a wonderful experience and told him that I was looking forward to learning more. Smiling at my response, he shared that he was looking for more women who would be interested in learning about firearms. He told me that he was impressed with the number of questions I asked and my enthusiasm to learn. He asked if I would be interested in taking an instructor's class. I told him I would have to think about it. When I mentioned it to my boyfriend that evening, he said he thought it was a great idea and suggested we take the training together.

We began spending most weekends at the club, attended meetings, and became a part of the community. Everyone was very welcoming and respectful. I began to notice that when my boyfriend wasn't next to me, he was never far away and was watching my every move. He would question me about conversations I was having and what once seemed like protective behavior began to feel more possessive and clingier.

During one of the meetings, the vice president of the club stood up to address the room about club safety rules and protocol. There was something so familiar about this man. I simply could not take my eyes off of him. He had an air of self-confidence that I was very attracted to. I found myself hanging on to his every word. At one point I had to remind myself that I was sitting next to my boyfriend and pull myself back from the hypnotic hold he seemed to have over me. I heard him mention that the club would be hosting the instructors training and that if anyone was interested, to speak to him.

When the meeting was over, I approached him to ask about the class. My boyfriend and I signed up. The first day of class, I walked into a room full of men and one other woman. I walked toward her and introduced myself. She had a very sweet demeanor, and I decided to take the seat next to her. My boyfriend began to object, insisting that he wanted me to sit with him. I told him that I felt more comfortable sitting with another woman and suggested he take a seat on the other side of the room.

I was beginning to feel as if I never had a moment just to myself. I wanted this to be something that I did without him breathing down my neck. I didn't want to hurt his feelings, but I needed some space.

The class was very intense and informative. I was pleased with the structure and strictness of it. I found that I was becoming more and more comfortable as I gained more knowledge in this new world. The more I learned, the more I realized there was so much more I would have to know. I found it intellectually stimulating and exciting. I was enjoying a surge of independence.

Slowly, I began to see my boyfriend in a world where he was interacting with others and not just with me. There were moments that I began to truly question why I was with this man. I started to notice tendencies that he had that were making me feel uneasy. He always seemed to be too close by. I had very little time alone, and quite honestly, it was triggering some past memories of being controlled and abused. He was not abusive, but I was feeling a little suffocated.

While we were home studying for the written exams, he became very distracting, which I considered disrespectful to my learning process. I wanted to have time alone to study, so I began looking for ways to put some distance between us. I was very focused and determined to complete the course with high scores for my own peace of mind and personal satisfaction.

On the day of the exam, once the written part was complete, we moved to the range for the practical exam target qualification. I was anxious as we had only one chance to qualify. Patiently, I waited my turn to set up my target. I was breathing and focused, waiting for the signal to begin.

I heard a familiar voice behind me, jokingly say, "Do you think I can make her jump?"

I held my focus and thought to myself, I don't think so! A second later, the command came, and I fired. I had three shots, and they were all in the bull's eye. I cleared my firearm, laid it down on the bench, turned, and came face-to-face with the vice president. He smiled at me and said, "Nice grouping."

My heart skipped a beat, and I felt my entire body begin to melt. What was it about this man that affected me so much? My boyfriend quickly positioned himself between us and broke the spell.

After becoming certified as instructors, we became more involved in club events. The vice president was in charge of most events, and my boyfriend seemed to want to befriend him. He volunteered us for everything that was requested. In my boyfriend's attempts to become his friend, we also became friendly. I was becoming very comfortable with him and continued to find him wildly attractive. He had a wonderfully sarcastic, flirtatious sense of humor that I found irresistible.

He invited us to participate in an event hosted by the club. It was the same event that introduced me to firearms, and we were both excited to be included. On the day of the event, I was placed as one of the instructors on the pistol station, and the vice president was running the rifle station, located right next to where I was. My boyfriend was sent to work with the shotguns at the other end of the grounds.

After the event, as we were cleaning up our stations, I looked up and saw the vice president walking down range towards the targets, rifle in hand. There was something about his energy, confidence, and intelligence that captivated me. His very presence affected me. What was it about this man that was so familiar?

I saw him take his rifle and begin moving it through the air in practiced, graceful arcs. The rifle became an extension of his arms, and his steps were skilled and graceful. I realized he was the Kung Fu Sifu! I started to laugh. Suddenly it made sense to me why he was so familiar. I spent hours watching and studying this man's movements, admiring him through the observation window years before. There he was, wielding his rifle as if it were his broad sword.

When we got back to the club, I mentioned to him that I enjoyed watching him practice forms with his rifle. He just looked at me quizzically and said, "How do you know that?"

I just said, "Wah Lum Kung Fu."

His response was, "Why do you know that name?"

I told him, "Because I was in the Tai Chi class that came after yours, and I used to watch you through the observation window."

He just laughed and said, "I don't remember you."

I smiled and said, "I know, but I remember you."

My boyfriend seemed threatened and unhappy. What I thought was protectiveness quickly turned to possessiveness and jealousy that I had something in common with someone other than himself. Witnessing the actions and antics of my boyfriend, attempting to gain his attention and friendship, was causing me to truly take a step back. He was beginning to show signs of insecurity and the need to be the center of attention. I began to question our relationship. Had I settled into what I thought was a normal relationship? If I were truly happy why, was I so attracted to another man?

One night a group of us were sitting by a bonfire at the club. I caught a glimpse of movement through the leaves just past the light of the flames. A figure appeared at the edge of the clearing. He stood there silently, unnoticed by anyone but me. I recognized his stealthy movements and air of confidence and smiled at his sudden appearance. There was something about his presence that soothed my soul and, at the same time, caused my heart to leap with excitement. The world seemed to fade away, and I could see only him. I thought maybe it was the moonshine they had been passing around, but the reaction I had every time he was near ran deep within me and lingered well after we parted ways. He had always had this effect on me from the moment I saw him through the window at the Kung Fu school.

On the fourth of July, my boyfriend and I were invited to a party that the vice president was hosting. There was a large group of people eating, drinking, and enjoying the festivities of the day. I was in the kitchen looking for a wine opener when he walked in. He gently took the bottle of wine from my hands and opened it. I was standing so close to him that I could feel the warmth of his body. As I turned to thank him, he leaned down and gently kissed my lips. His kiss took my breath away; it felt as if fireworks were exploding throughout my entire body. I grabbed onto the island in front of me for balance. In the blink of an eye, he was gone. I could hear his voice beyond the door on the deck. I stood there for a moment, trying to regain my composure. That night, as I lay in bed, all I could think was, "Dear God, please do not let me die without having him kiss me again."

After the party, I began distancing myself from my boyfriend in public and pulling away from him in private. We had stopped having sex. I had gained a few pounds, starting a bad cycle of stress eating. I mentioned to him one night at dinner that we should talk about what was happening in our relationship. His response was, "You have gained weight, and I no longer find you attractive."

He was unusually cold and cruel in his statement. I suddenly felt self-conscious and unattractive. It felt as if my stomach dropped through the floor. I was sad that the person I was sharing my life with found it so easy to speak to me this way. I became very quiet for the rest of the evening, feeling very self-conscious, ashamed, and hurt. My mind was racing. I was fearful of what I would say to this man who was living in my home, sleeping in my bed, and thought it was ok to speak to me so disrespectfully.

The next day, I was on the phone with the vice president, talking about a firearms class I had attended. I wanted his professional opinion about some of the training methods that were used. We talked for a while, and I thanked him for his time. Before we hung up, he said he noticed sadness in my voice and asked if I was ok. I was not ok.

He asked me what had happened, and I told him what my boyfriend said to me the night before. He let out a belly laugh, saying, "Your boyfriend is an idiot. You are incredibly beautiful. There is something wrong with him. I honestly don't understand why you are with this guy."

Upon hearing the sincerity in his voice, tears began streaming down my cheeks. I thanked him for his advice and kind words, and then hung up. I had some serious soul searching to do.

I knew that I had to lose some weight to feel better and be healthier. I also knew that I had been stress eating because I was unhappy. I was feeling insecure. My boyfriend chose to shame me instead of loving me, and that was simply not acceptable.

I called Sifu later that week and shared with him what had happened. He said that he thought my boyfriend was cruel for saying that to me, and he didn't understand why I was with him. After hearing that statement twice in one week, I admitted he was right. It was time for me to end the relationship.

Hearing this, he said, "Well, maybe now you will finally give me a chance."

Hearing him say those words made me laugh. He had said that to me so many times over the years that it always made me feel loved. I never, for a moment, thought he was serious, but it was always wonderful to feel wanted. I told him that "I appreciated him more than he could ever know."

The next day, I told my boyfriend that I had thought about what he said to me, and I felt it was time to go our separate ways. My words caught him so off guard that he started to back pedal. Stuttering, he said, "No, really, all I meant was maybe if we went to the gym together and worked out, it would be better."

I told him that it was over. I realized that I had not been happy for quite some time, and we owed it to ourselves to find people that we were attracted to and happy with.

I would have thrown him out that night if not for the fact that his children had become a part of our household on the weekends. That would not be fair to them, so I held myself back for the moment. I needed a chance to calm down and process what had just happened. I told him that he needed to find somewhere else to live, and until then, he was to leave my room and sleep on the couch in the basement.

He mistakenly thought that I would get over my decision and took his time looking for a place to live, using the excuse that there was just nothing available in the area that he could afford. Every now and then, he would ask if there was any way to work it out. He professed his love for me and apologized for hurting me. His treatment of me was unforgivable, and his apologies rang empty in my ears. My heart began to grow cold toward him.

The One

The day I shared with the vice president what my boyfriend had said about my weight and his lack of attraction towards me, his response made me feel safe and cared for. I considered him a friend, yet I was intensely attracted to this man. The thought that he, in any small way, was also attracted to me made my mind race and my heart soar. Wild fantasies of what it would be like to be with him filled my thoughts; his mere presence affected me.

After that day he would call just to say hello and see how I was feeling. We met a few times for coffee and walks in a nearby park. When we spoke, he listened intently and never broke eye contact. Having someone's undivided attention is a unique experience. It is rare to have a level of communication that goes beyond listening—not to simply respond, but to truly hear another person.

From the moment I set eyes on him, I was inexplicably drawn to him. The first time I saw him at the Kung Fu school through the observation glass, then again when I was in the audience at the club, he captivated me. He had an air of confidence about him that commanded attention, and his voice was unique and hypnotic.

Each time he turned his gaze towards me, it was as if he could see me—truly see me. When he stood close, I could feel his energy reaching out to me. I had to consciously keep myself from leaning into him and making physical contact. The air between us seemed to have an electric charge that made my skin tingle and my heart race. I had never truly believed in soul mates until I met this man.

He would offer suggestions when I asked for his advice, but he never attempted to tell me what to do. As a natural teacher and mentor, I recognized that this was a man of honor and integrity. He possessed personal power that I admired, and he respected my own innate power without any kind of possessiveness.

One evening he called and asked me out for a drink. As we sat in the booth across from each other, he reached over the table and touched my hand. That simple physical contact made me smile, and I felt as if he had reached into my soul and touched me. We sat at a secluded booth, had a few appetizers and cocktails as we chatted. Time seemed to stand still; I could not remember ever feeling quite so at ease with someone. He walked me to my car, and as we were saying goodnight, he leaned in to kiss me.

He placed a warm hand at the nape of my neck and tilted my face up as he slowly lowered his face towards mine. I could almost feel the warmth of his lips touch mine with anticipation. I felt lightheaded just being this close to this man. He gently and slowly leaned in and placed his lips on mine. I opened my mouth slightly in response to him, and I felt a strong arm slide around my body and hold me closer. My legs went weak for a moment as he held me in his arms. I rested my head just below his shoulder and felt as if we were somehow cast from the same mold. Our bodies fit together perfectly in that sweet embrace.

He opened the car door for me, smiled, and told me that he would call me. I sat in the car for a few moments, not trusting my senses to be able to drive. That night I climbed into bed, the memory of his lips touching mine, and fell into a deep, delicious slumber.

The next evening, he called. As usual we fell into an effortless conversation. His job and work schedule had him travelling from early Monday mornings until Friday evenings. He told me that he would be arriving home late Friday night but would like to see me Saturday if I was free. I had plans with a friend Saturday evening, but I told him that I would be free in the afternoon if that worked for him. I did my best to contain my excitement that he wanted to see me again.

That week it became a ritual for him to call me in the evening when he got back to his hotel room and was settling in to sleep. One night our conversation turned to the goodnight kiss we shared. He told me that he thought about it often. I felt my pulse race a little, and I freely admitted how much I enjoyed kissing him. After a short while, our conversation shifted from friendly accounts of the day to flirtatious descriptions of how it would be to kiss each other goodnight if we were together.

Each night our conversations became more detailed and comfortable than the last. After carefully listening to each other's responses, we began to learn about each other. We took turns describing how we envisioned ourselves kissing, caressing, and exploring each other without ever touching, as we lay in our own separate beds.

By the end of the week, I had become so comfortable with him that when I heard his voice, I would simply close my eyes, and it was as if he were lying beside me. I was captivated by his descriptions of how he wanted to touch me, bringing vivid images to life in my mind. He was romantic and seductive. I was spellbound. He was awakening in me a longing for passion and sensuality that I had suppressed.

Saturday finally came. I heard the doorbell ring and had to force myself to walk slowly to answer it. As I walked down the stairs to the front door, my heart was racing. I opened the door and was greeted by his warm smile. I invited him in, and as I closed the door, without a word, he took me in his arms and kissed me passionately. I felt myself respond to his touch so completely that we never even made it up the stairs. The week of hot phone conversations felt as if we had already made love without ever touching.

As I ran my hands down his arms, I felt his strong muscles holding me tightly to his body; I felt lightheaded and was wildly turned on. The skirt I was wearing gave him easy access to me, and as I felt the warmth of his hands touching me, my breath quickened. I felt him hard and ready as I unzipped his jeans. We were still on the steps when I felt him enter into me. He was perfect, and I could think of nothing except wanting to please him.

Like a sweet explosion, I felt him come inside me. Filled with intense emotion, I felt tears of pure joy welling up in my eyes and quickly wiped them away so he would not see. I was overwhelmed and breathless. I gently took his hand and walked him to my bed. We undressed and lay in each other's arms without saying a word.

He began to run his hands over my body, caressing every part of me gently and knowingly, as if he had been making love to me for a lifetime. He admired my curves and began kissing me deeply on the mouth, and then he moved slowly to the nape of my neck. My breath once again quickened as I felt my skin tingling from his touch. As his warm mouth began sliding down my stomach, I let him know that he had me very close to climaxing again, and he said, "That was my intention."

I was concerned about pleasuring him, but he assured me that satisfying me meant much more to him. I felt his warm breath just before his tongue skillfully teased my clit. I grabbed onto his shoulders harder than I intended, and he pulled away. I didn't want him to stop. I quickly apologized and begged him not to stop. I had never been the one who was the focus of affection.

He bowed his head once more, bringing me back immediately to a place of excitement I had never known, and I completely surrendered to him. My breathing was heavy, and my body was vibrating as he skillfully brought me to the sweetest, most intense orgasm I had ever experienced. I felt my body go limp as he took me in his arms and held me.

We lay together, our naked bodies entwined. I was once again overwhelmed with emotion, tears returned to my eyes, but this time I could not hide them. Concerned, he asked, "Are you alright?" I just smiled and assured him that they were happy tears as he cradled me in his arms.

Once again, I was struck at how perfectly our bodies fit together. I truly felt as if I was made just for him. I closed my eyes, sweetly satisfied, and drifted off into a light sleep. After a short while, he said that he had to go and hoped that we could see each other again soon. All I could think was that I never wanted him to leave.

I walked him to the door, and as I watched him walk to his car, I prayed he would look back one more time. He opened the car door, looked up, and smiled at me. This incredible man had touched my heart in a way that could either destroy me or bring me to a place of love that I had never known. I decided that he was worth the risk, as I felt all of the walls I had built up over the years to protect myself simply crumble the moment he smiled at me.

Weeks passed, and we fell into a very comfortable and exciting routine of speaking every day. He began calling during the day if he had a moment, and every night to share our days and say goodnight. Our nightly conversations seamlessly slid into seductive descriptions of the anticipation of our weekends when we would finally have time to be together.

I loved the fact that he was truly independent. He appreciated that I was fine with his travelling for work and thrilled to find me waiting for him to return on weekends. The more time we spent together, the more comfortable we became, and our passion for one another grew. He continued to encourage desires and the natural sensuality that I had become so desperately frightened of showing.

One of the things that I found so intensely attractive about this man was his sense of security. He did not appear to have a jealous bone in his body. He made me feel as if I was the only woman in the world, yet he was not at all possessive. He assured me that he had no desire to control me. If I wanted or needed to travel, he would be there waiting for me, as I did for him, to return. He encouraged me to step into my own personal power fully and completely. This was a new experience for me. I had never been with someone who was not attempting to reign in my energy or control me.

The one stumbling block that we were facing was that my ex-boyfriend was still sleeping in my basement on the couch. He was taking his time finding someplace else to live, and I was finding it difficult to throw him out because of his children. My new boyfriend made it clear that he was not happy about him being there. He felt I was being taken advantage of, and he was right. He offered to figure out a way to make it clear that it was time for him to go, assuring me that he would take care of it, and I felt relieved.

The Dinner Party

My boyfriend was out of town for work. We made plans that Friday for him to come over, cook dinner, and enjoy a quiet night together. The Match date was still living in the basement and showing no effort to leave. He kept using his children as an excuse to stay, asking if there was any chance of us getting back together. I was becoming irritated with him for being disrespectful of my request for him to leave. Impatiently, I told him there was no chance for us ever again. I let him know that he would need to make other arrangements for that Friday evening as I had dinner plans. I wanted the house to myself.

The next night, I received a phone call from Sifu. I had not heard from him since I told him what had happened with the Match date; he was calling to let me know that he was coming to town. I realized that he would assume he had a place to stay at my house, and perhaps more so since he knew that I had broken up with the match date. Since we had not spoken, he did not know about my new boyfriend or that they knew each other.

My worlds were about to collide. I had told my new boyfriend about my relationship with Sifu when I realized they knew each other. I did not want there to be any surprises. I explained that we were dear friends, who at times were more than that given the circumstances through the years. He assured me that since we were committed to being exclusive, he trusted me and understood that Sifu and I were friends. His only response was that he hadn't seen or spoken to him for fifteen years. He did not seem to have any issues with him or our relationship. His confidence, trust, and absence of jealousy were foreign to me and wonderfully attractive.

I called Sifu and told him that I had met someone and was falling quite hard and fast. When he asked who it was, I said his name, and Sifu began yelling at me. He had never, in the fifteen years we had known one another, raised his voice to me. He accused me of betraying him. I had no idea what he was talking about, but the more I insisted I didn't know, the louder he yelled and accused me of being a liar.

I was so furious that I yelled back and hung up the phone. After all these years and so many relationships between us, we have always been supportive and caring of each other. We have only treated each other with love, respect, and compassion. I was caught completely off guard. I don't lie, and I certainly have never lied to him.

I was hurt, angry, and confused. I called my boyfriend to ask him if he had any idea what Sifu was talking about. He told me that he had no idea and that he didn't have a problem with him. Sifu and I had shared so much together over the years. For him to treat me that way was simply devastating. I told my boyfriend that I was ready to walk away from my friendship with Sifu, and he insisted that there was no way to end such a long friendship.

He told me to call him back and invite him to dinner that Friday night so they could talk and clear the air. I agreed and called Sifu, telling him what my boyfriend had said, and he agreed to come. We made plans for me to pick him up at his mom's house and bring him home. We had some time to visit; he seemed much calmer. He said that he believed me when I told him I had no idea why he reacted that way, yet he still would not tell me why. At this point I assumed that whatever it was had nothing to do with me. They would work it out over dinner. I was still feeling hurt that he would treat me that way. I felt myself feeling guarded in our conversation for the first time.

My boyfriend called to let me know that he was on his way home; he was picking up a few things for dinner. He told me to tell Sifu that he was looking forward to their reunion. A few minutes after that phone call, the Match date called to say that he was on his way back to the house. He told me that he had his daughter and a friend of hers with him, and they had no place to go for a few hours. I reminded him that I was going to have company, and he asked if they could join us. I called my boyfriend, and he said it would be fine; he would just pick up some extra food.

My mind was racing as I imagined all three of them sitting around my dinner table. The one thing these three men had in common besides me was their apparent alarming lack of boundaries. The other thing that all three men shared was their intense protective nature towards children, especially girls. This was a blessing in disguise, as I knew that any embarrassing topics would not come up with the girls at the table.

My boyfriend was the last to arrive, with groceries in hand. After he put everything in the kitchen, he politely greeted the Match date, his daughter, and her friend. He turned towards me and kissed me deeply as he wrapped me in a warm embrace, then shook Sifu's hand, stating it was good to see him after all those years.

They were cordial with one another and chatted for a moment as friends who had not seen each other in years. My boyfriend excused himself and headed straight for the kitchen to start cooking dinner. I set the table and checked in with my boyfriend to see if he needed anything, and he assured me that he had everything under control. He seemed to be enjoying himself while cooking dinner and told me everything would be fine. He kissed me on the forehead and opened a bottle of wine for me to put on the table.

As we all gathered at the table, I could feel tension building. I looked at each one of their faces and realized there was an enormous amount of competitive energy in the air. My first concern was Sifu; he was unusually quiet and barely made eye contact with me or anyone else, for that matter. Although he knew everything about the match date, they had never met face-to-face. I knew that he wasn't happy that he was still living in my home, and I was once again grateful that the girls were at the table.

Next, my attention moved across the table to the Match date. I realized that he had no idea who Sifu was and most likely thought he was simply an old friend of my boyfriends. Clueless of the circumstances, he attempted to make light conversation. He was positioned next to his daughter and her friend, who were blissfully unaware of the drama unfolding before their eyes.

I kept telling myself, just breathe. My boyfriend entered the dining room with a smile on his face and a twinkle in his eyes. He served a delicious shrimp scampi nestled on top of perfectly cooked linguini. He took the seat next to me. His energy was calm and secure, and he seemed somewhat amused.

He focused his attention on the girls across the table. He was charming and playful with them, and they responded in kind. Being the center of their attention seemed to annoy the Match date, and I watched as he attempted to join in on the conversation, only to be skillfully excluded as my boyfriend continued to dominate the interaction.

Sifu continued to sit quietly at the end of the table, observing this interaction. I watched as he began to relax a little, realizing that my boyfriend's attention was entirely focused on the girls and my ex. At this point, I noticed him looking a little amused by the dynamics of this unusual dinner party. He smiled a little and gave me a look that confirmed how lucky I was that the girls were at the table. Realizing that the Match date was unaware of the dynamics at the table, Sifu was content to silently observe. My boyfriend, secure, confident, and in control of the evening, gave me the chance to relax a little.

Once again, I looked around the table at the faces of each of these men. First, the Match date. I listened as he attempted to interject into the conversation the girls were having with my boyfriend. I watched his insecurity grow as they ignored him. I noticed my boyfriend's conversation becoming even more playful and animated in response to the discomfort it was causing the Match date.

I realized that a large part of my relationship with the Match date had been him wanting and needing to be the center of attention. I wondered how I had stayed in that relationship for so long. As I looked at him, I remembered his subtle and not-so-subtle criticisms of me during the time we spent together. I felt as if the veil had been pulled back, and I saw him as he truly was for the first time. I sat back for a moment and thought, what did I ever see in this man?

Dinner ended, and everyone thanked my boyfriend for a delicious meal. The Match date left to drive his daughter and her friend home. It was getting late, so I told my boyfriend that I was going to drive Sifu back to his mom's. To my knowledge, they had still not spoken about whatever it was that caused him to accuse me of betrayal. I decided that whatever it was, it had nothing to do with me.

Civil yet cool with each other, they shook hands. My boyfriend walked us to the car, and as we got in, he had Sifu roll down the window. I watched as he locked eyes with him, and I heard him say in an intense, commanding, and slightly menacing tone, "She is going to drop you off and come right home. Do you understand?"

Sifu responded with a rather subdued "Yes."

Then he looked at me and smiled warmly, making me feel safe and cared for by saying, "I will be here when you get back."

As I began to pull out of the driveway and away from the house, I felt Sifu fully relax for the first time that evening. With a smug grin on his face, he playfully began to tease me about the relationships with the three men sitting around the table that night. I knew where he was going, and I pulled the car over. I looked at him and said, "You can stop right there. Think for just one second before you say another word. Yes, I slept with each one of you. You may all know me, but consider this: I know all of you. How would you like to sit here and listen to me make comparisons between you?" I then gave him the option of walking home if he said another word about it. He kept his comments to himself, and graciously accepted the ride home.

We rode in silence for the next twenty minutes. I knew in my heart that he had crossed a line that we would never be able to come back from. When we arrived, without saying a word, he opened the door to get out of the car.

I asked him if he was going to say goodbye, and his response was, "You need to go home; your boyfriend is expecting you." He left the car, walked away, and never looked back.

As I watched him leave, I knew that I would never see him again.

When I arrived back home, the Match date's car was in the driveway, and my boyfriend was waiting for me. He smiled at me confidently and took me into his arms in a warm and loving embrace. He kissed me deeply and passionately, which melted the sadness I felt over how Sifu treated me. He took me into the bedroom and told me to wait there for him; he had something he wanted to take care of.

I heard his footsteps on the stairs heading for the basement, then, after a few moments, he returned with a smile on his face, clearly amused. He told me that he went downstairs to ask my ex if he had his hearing protection that he used on the firing range available. When he answered yes, he suggested he use it because it was going to get loud upstairs. I simply burst out laughing. With surgical precision, he cleared the playing field and won my heart.

Destiny

After the dinner party, the Match date moved out, and my boyfriend began staying over more often. He continued to travel during the week, and on weekends, he would come and stay with me. We spoke every day, and each night he would call to share his day, listen to mine, and sometimes fall asleep together on the phone.

I loved hearing about his adventures on the road. I admired his passion and work ethics. He was one of the hardest working men I had ever met. He would tell me how much he missed me and ask about my day and the things that I was working on. He was always encouraging and supportive of me.

The more I got to know him, the more he surprised me. He was accomplished in so many areas and humble about each. I was in love with him, but more than that, I liked him as a person. He made me smile, laugh, and feel as if I were the most beautiful woman he had ever known. I had never felt this safe or happy in a relationship.

After a few months, he suggested that we move in together. We each owned our own homes, and he wanted me to decide where we would live. I lived in a split-level ranch on a lovely corner lot in a small town, and he had a cape-style home on beautifully landscaped property. He told me that he had built the house and landscaped the yard himself.

The house was set up on a hill. Guarding the entrance of the long driveway stood a red maple tree accented with beautiful lemon-colored irises and surrounded by a lovely hand-stacked stone wall. At the top of the driveway was a mound that looked like an English garden, with various colors and a wide variety of glorious flowers.

I gazed across the front lawn, and it looked like a lush green carpet with a small section of mulch and trees to one side. To my delight, he told me it was a small orchard with apples, pears, peaches, and a cherry tree. I could almost taste the fresh fruit as I imagined it all in full bloom.

He walked me through an arch of lilacs that stood seven feet high across a small stone walk that reminded me of an entrance to a secret garden. We emerged onto a small patch of soft green grass, met by beautifully landscaped bushes and more flowers. In the back was a magnificent slate patio that he created, and just beyond that was a small rock river that was fed by the drains on the house under the patio.

Beyond the bushes was conservation land, so there would never be any homes built behind us. In the woods lived foxes, deer, coyotes, hawks, owls, and more. I loved the idea that animals and land would be protected. A small hand-built stone wall lined the back of the property that had been built in colonial days and, by law, could not be tampered with. I felt as if I had stepped on sacred land.

As we came around the back of the house on the opposite side of the yard, we saw a twenty-by-forty foot garden and eight large blueberry bushes. I was in awe. We had not even stepped foot into the house. I had made my decision.

From the outside, the house appeared to be a small cape house. To my surprise, when I walked in, I was met with an enormous kitchen. It had beautiful marble countertops with a large island in the middle. The ceiling was graced with three hanging Tiffany lamps. The cabinets were custom built with recessed lights under them, and there was a lovely built-in desk.

The downstairs had a dining room and a media room with surround sound and a custom-built media station. In the living room, there was a three-piece custom-designed mirror-backed showcase that housed a hand-built replica of the US Constitution. The living room also housed a stylish pellet stove. Upstairs, there were four bedrooms, each with a walk-in closet. There was a main full bath and a full bath in the master bedroom. The ceiling of the master bedroom had a skylight.

I knew that he had put his own blood, sweat, and tears into building this house and landscaping the yard. I loved every inch of it. It was as if he had built my dream house. The yard had everything I had always dreamed of, right down to the small red maple tree at the end of the driveway. There was no question in my mind—this was where we belonged.

I contacted my real estate agent, and we set a timeline to get my house ready to list for sale. Our goal was to sell my house and put most of the proceeds towards the mortgage on his home. He made arrangements to refinance the mortgage on his house with my name on it, as well as the deed, so I would be protected.

Three days after the house was listed, we received an offer above the asking price. I accepted the offer, and we closed a few weeks later. We decided that aside from the built-in cabinets in the media room and living room and the beautiful kitchen table and chairs he had built, we would start fresh with all the new furniture that we chose together.

Since he traveled during the week, I went to collect paint samples for each room while he was away, and when he came home on the weekend, we chose them together. Each room was painted and decorated in such a way that it complimented the one next to it. The flow and energy in the house became as comfortable and seamless as we were.

One night we were sitting in the living room, and he pulled out an old yearbook that contained old letters and memories. He shared with me a love letter that was written to him by a childhood sweetheart. It was innocent, sweet, and loving. I felt honored that he was sharing a softer, more romantic side of himself. I loved the fact that he cherished that sweet memory. I silently wished that I had memories of young, innocent love.

He continued to turn the pages in his yearbook and came upon a picture that made him smile. He pointed at it and said, "This was my favorite cousin."

I looked at the photograph and exclaimed, "I know him," and said his name. He was the cousin of my best friend in high school. Then I named off his cousin's mother and father as auntie and uncle, as well as his brother and sister.

He looked at me with wide eyes and said, "Are we cousins?"

"No." I corrected him. "I was best friends with their cousin and spent most of my high school summers at their home." Suddenly, I felt my world starting to fold in on me once again. My best friend in high school was the sister of my first boyfriend.

This was the beginning of many uncomfortable conversations we would share about our past. He wanted to know everything, as so many had before. Fear rose in my heart. Each time I shared my past, it always seemed to start the same way: with an understanding ear, then turning to control and sometimes abuse.

I hesitated, and when he looked into my eyes, I felt them fill with tears. He told me that there was nothing I could say that would make him stop loving me. He told me he only wanted the truth and for me to feel safe. I believed him and began to share my story. This time, and for the first time, I started from the beginning, revealing the secret and shame of my childhood experiences.

When I was done, I lay sobbing in his arms, feeling damaged and ashamed. How could he still love me? I kept my eyes cast down towards the floor, afraid to see him looking at me differently now that he knew everything. He placed his hand under my chin and lifted my face to look into his eyes. The light in them towards me had not changed.

He smiled gently and told me that I had nothing to be ashamed about. He assured me that the only thing he heard in my stories was that I had a loving heart and was taken advantage of. He saw me not as damaged but as a strong woman who refused to be broken. He said he saw me as having the power of a goddess and that he was honored to be loved by me.

That Christmas morning, under the tree, lay our gifts and our stockings. At the bottom of my stocking, I found a small blue velvet box. My hands began to tremble as I opened it. Nestled in the blue velvet box was the most incredible Ceylon sapphire ring, surrounded by diamonds. He asked me on bent knee to marry him. I was so surprised, I could hardly breathe. He told me I had to answer him. In my excitement, I did not realize that I had not said yes out loud! "Yes, yes, of course I will!" I answered. We opened a bottle of Prosecco to toast our future.

I looked out the window, and it was a clear, crisp day. Snowflakes began falling gently from the sky. As the grass became covered in a sparkling blanket of snow, I decided to share one more story with him. I told him that Christmas was always my favorite time of year. I shared with him that when I was a child, the family would wrap presents together to donate every year. The day the chief of police came to the house with his young nephew flashed sweetly in my mind.

He mentioned that when he was small, he and his uncle, the chief of police of the town we both grew up in, would ride around in his cruiser to pick up gifts. I started to laugh, realizing that he was the young boy who had come to my door so many years ago to pick up the gifts for Christmas donations. There was no question in my mind. He was my destiny.

Acknowledgements

I would like to thank, first and foremost, my husband. Without his encouragement, unconditional love, and support, this story would never have been told.

I would also like to thank my beautiful beta readers for their honest opinions and, above all, their time. Thank you to my "Staples Angel" for her assistance and her encouragement. Thank you to my "Lady Catherine" for her attention to detail in finding the title for this book. Thank you to my accountability partner for keeping me focused and on track, as well as for the hours we spent together sifting through the emotional editing.

I am grateful to each and every one of you for being a part of my journey.

Milton Keynes UK
Ingram Content Group UK Ltd.
UKHW050035190624
444315UK00015B/949